Walenty's

Tattoo Coloring Book

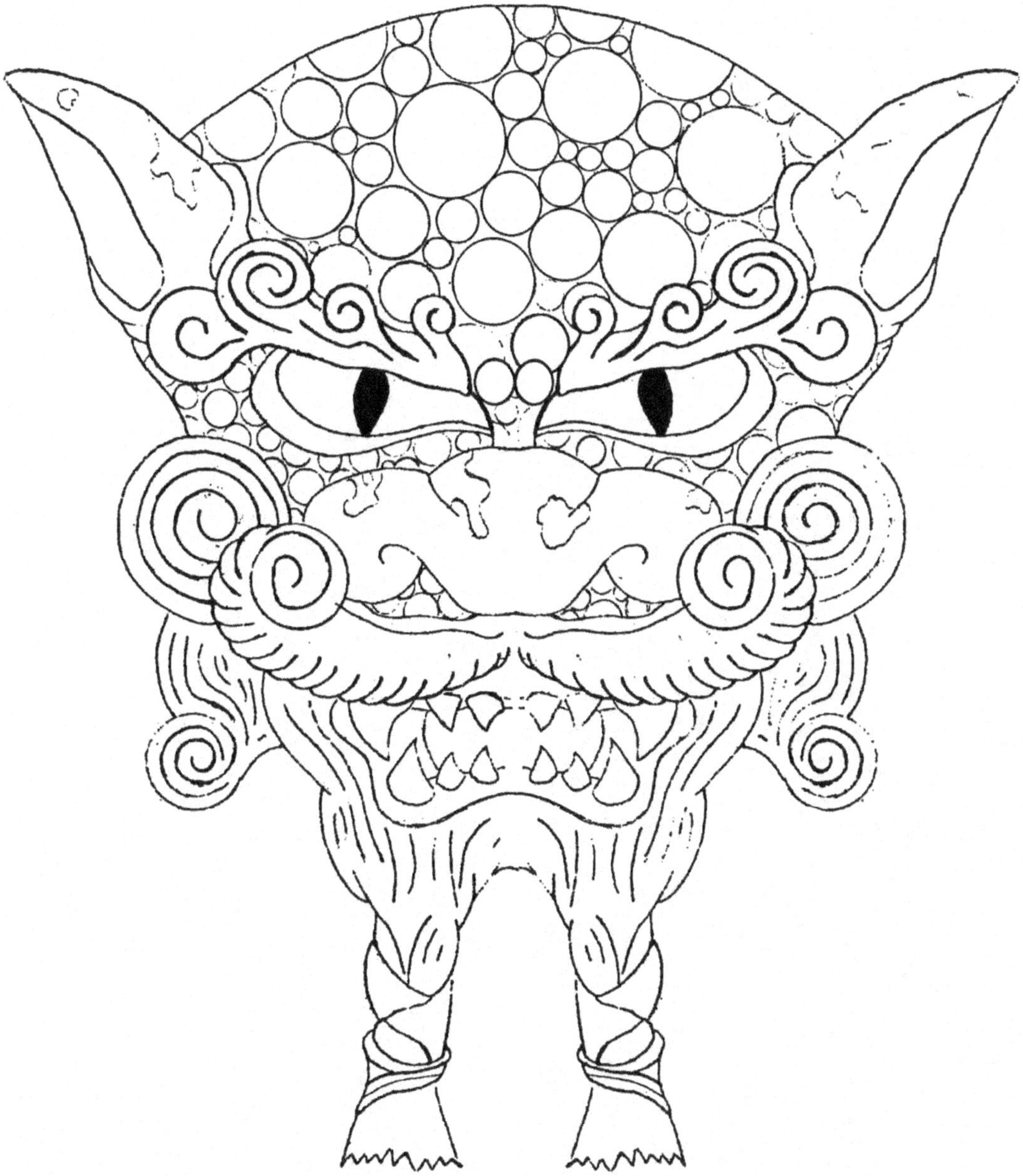

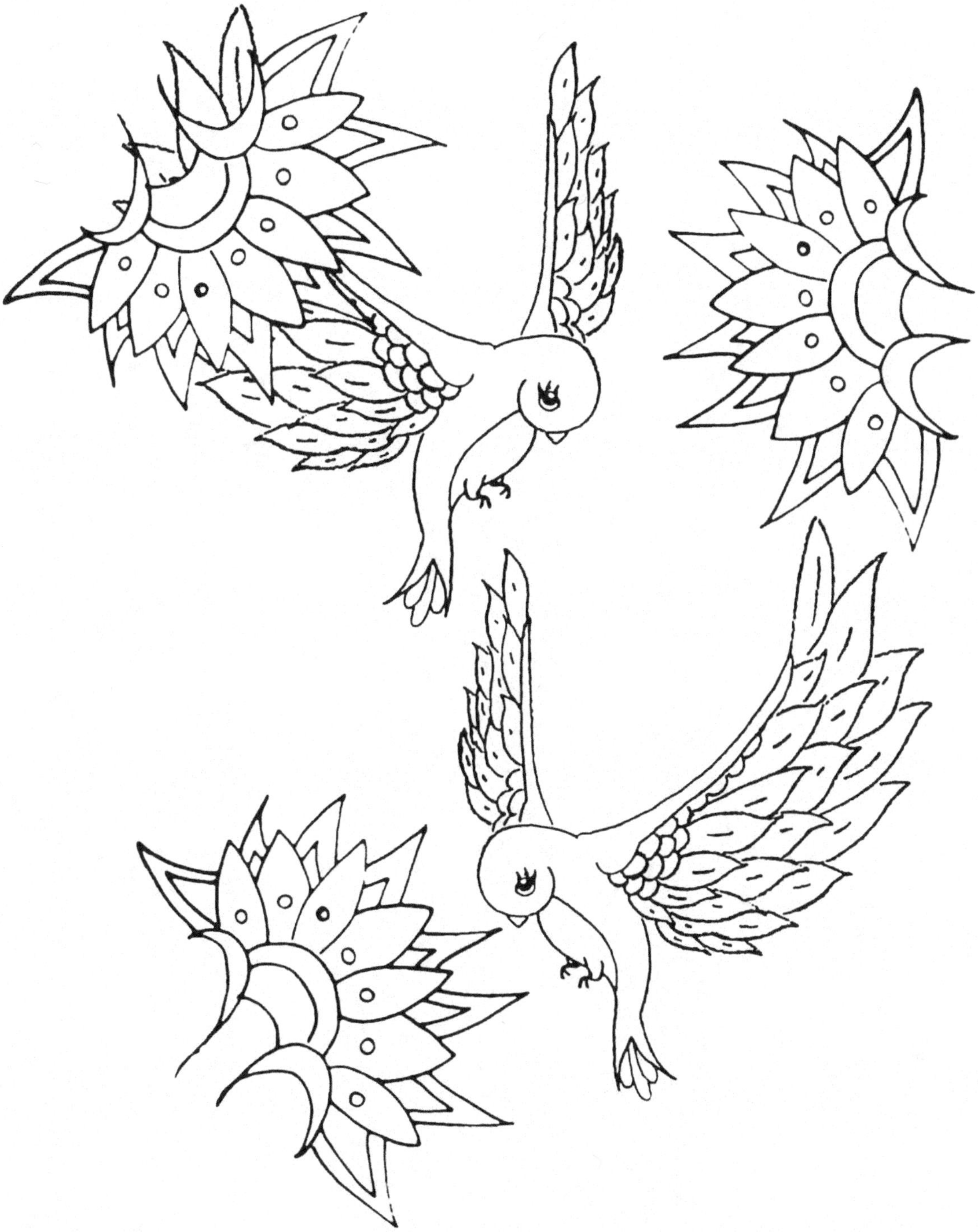

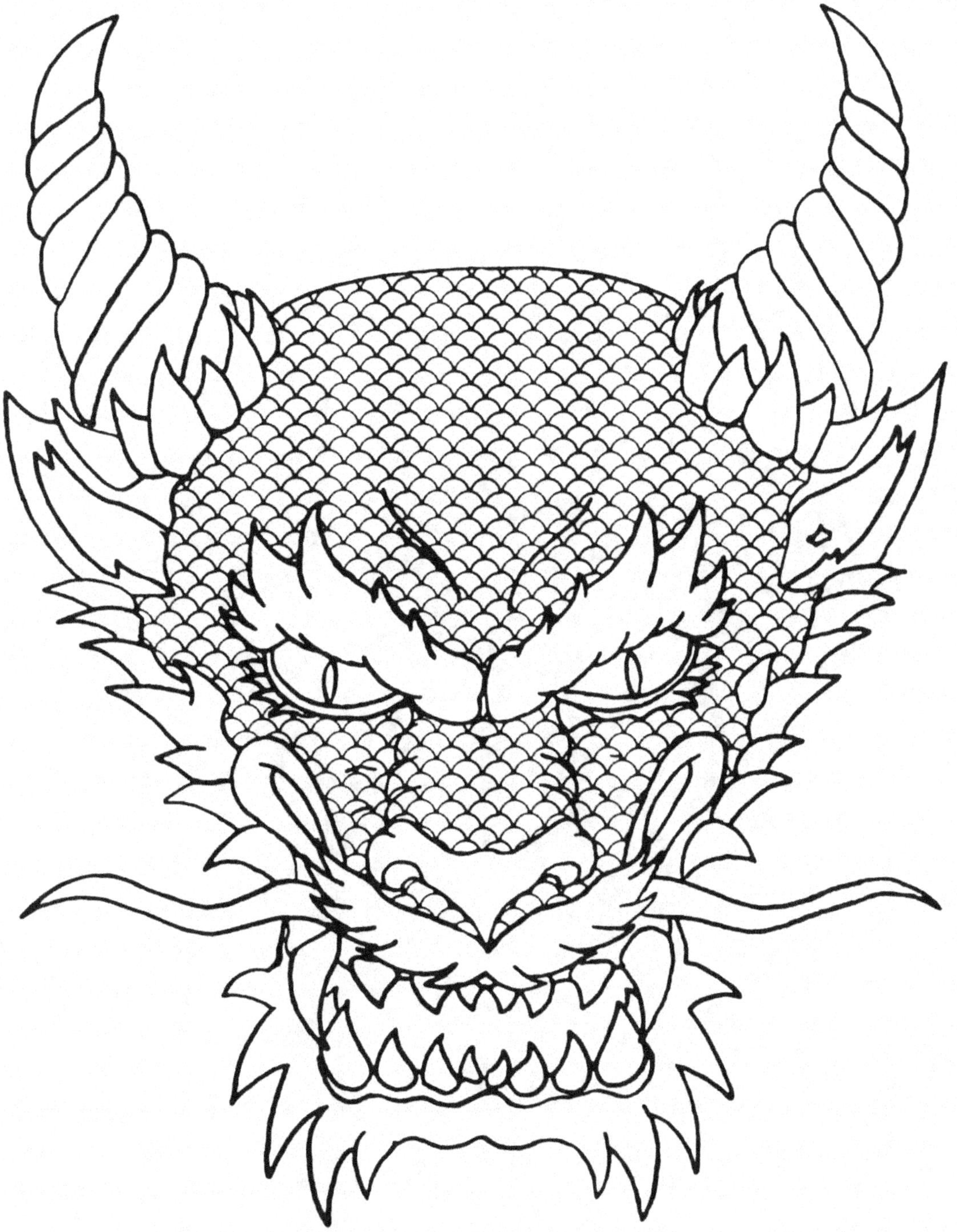

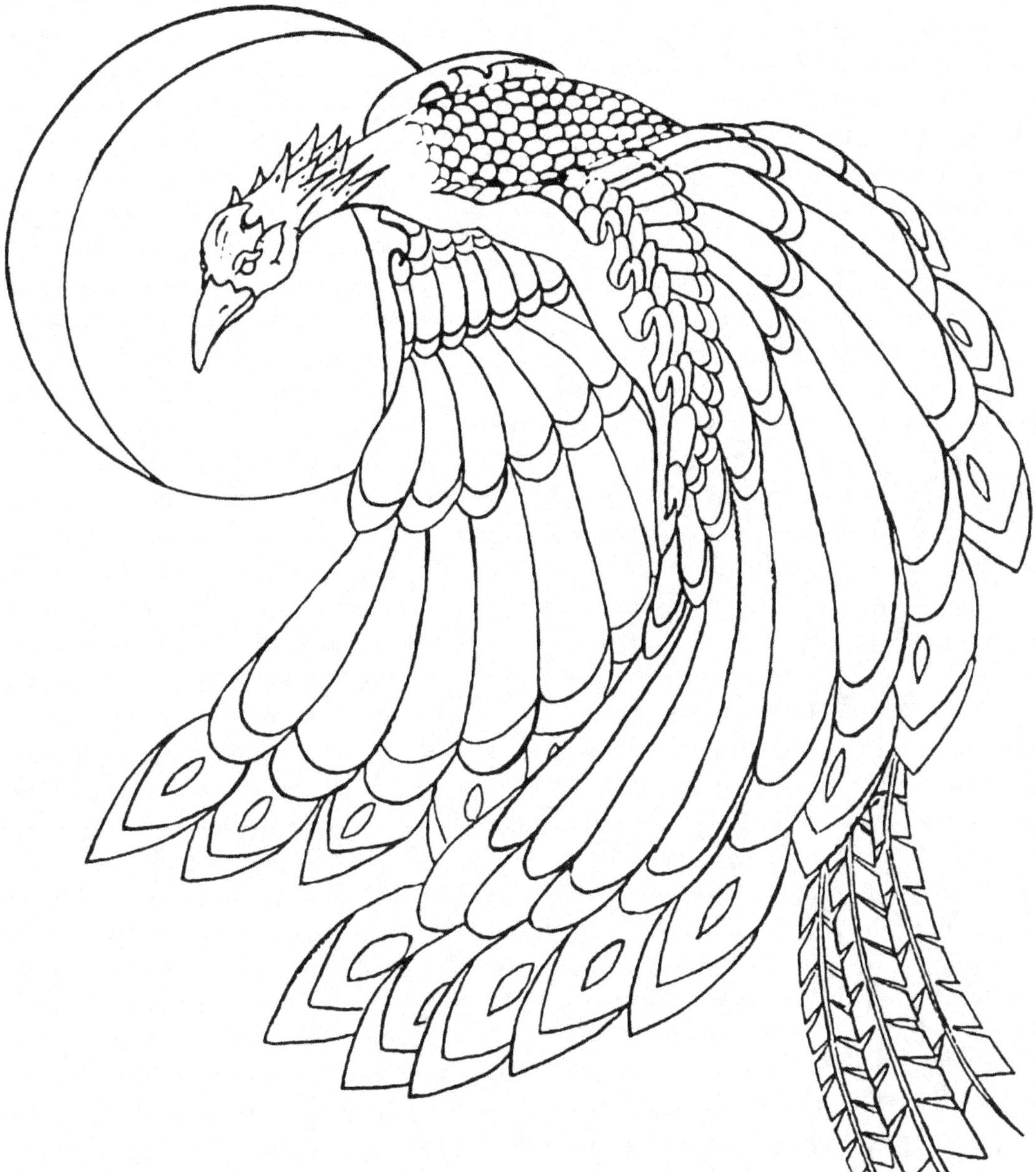

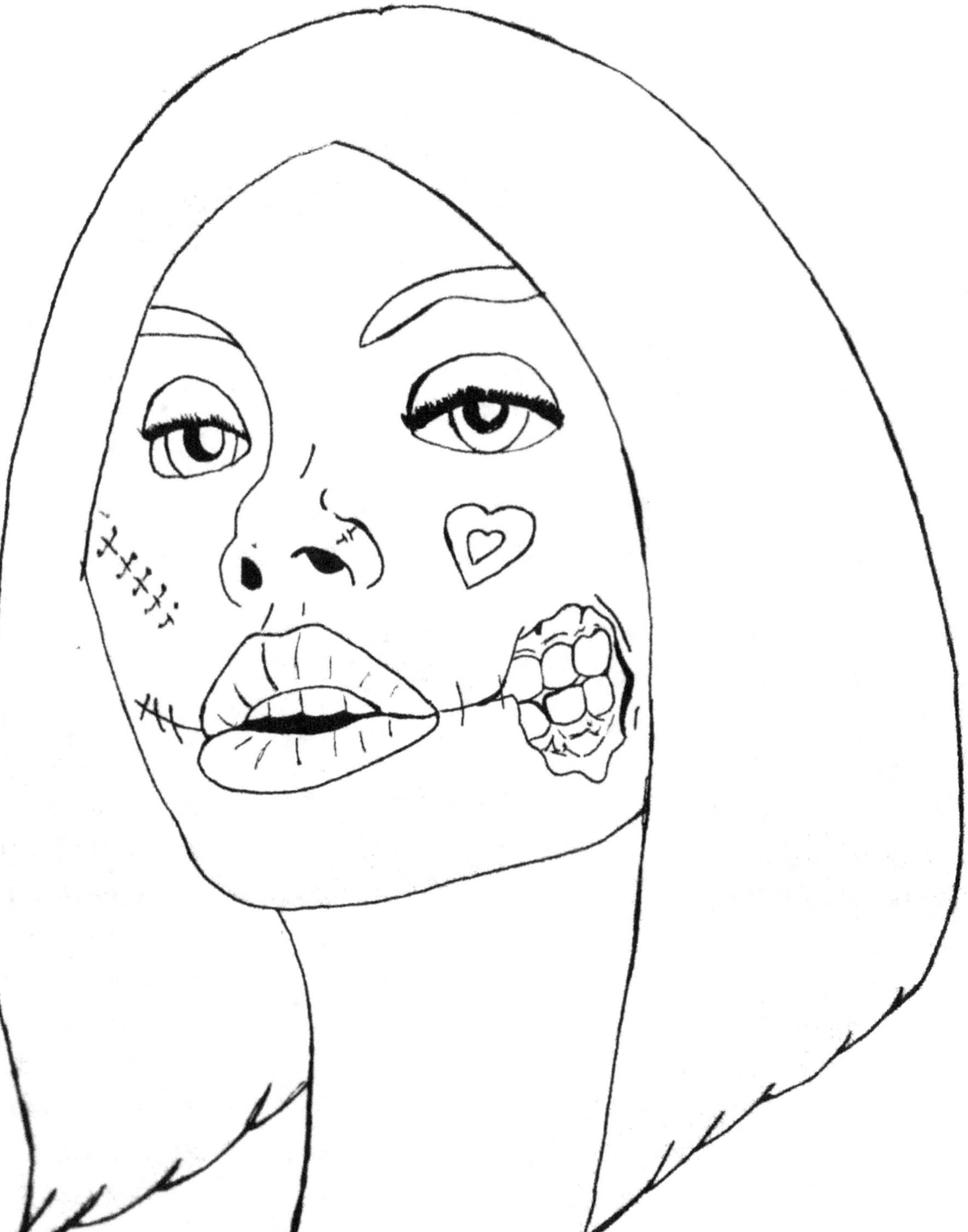

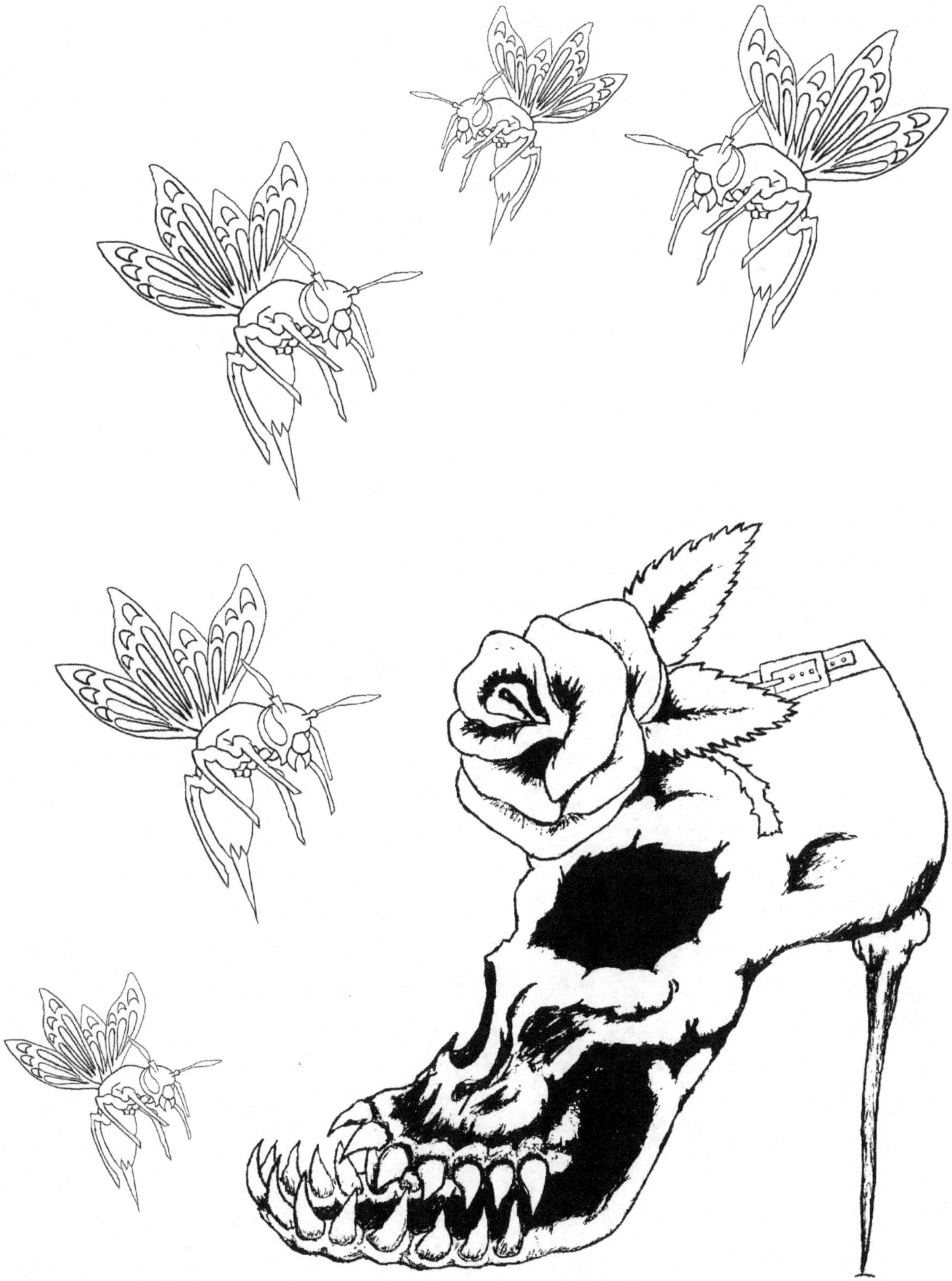

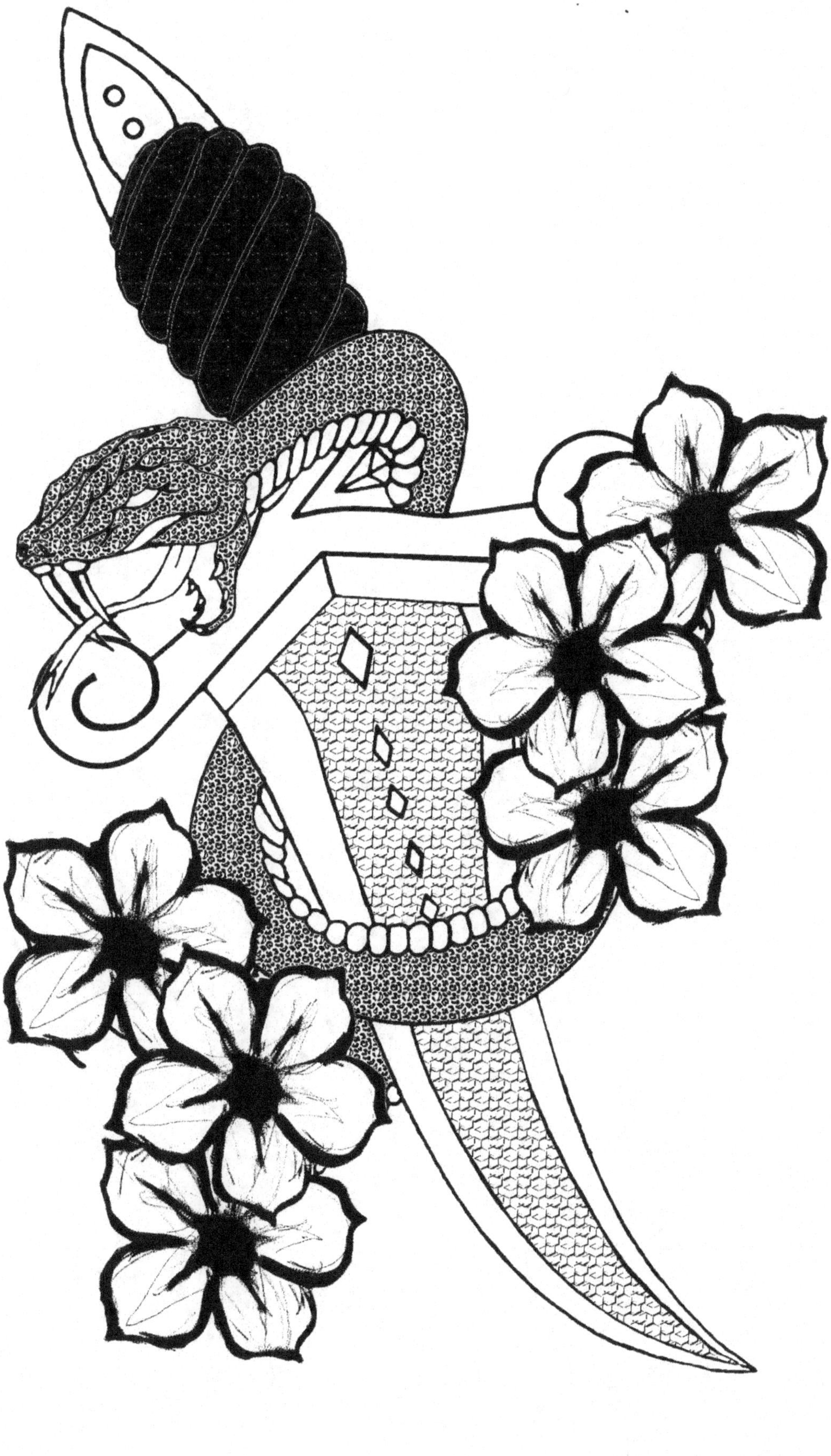

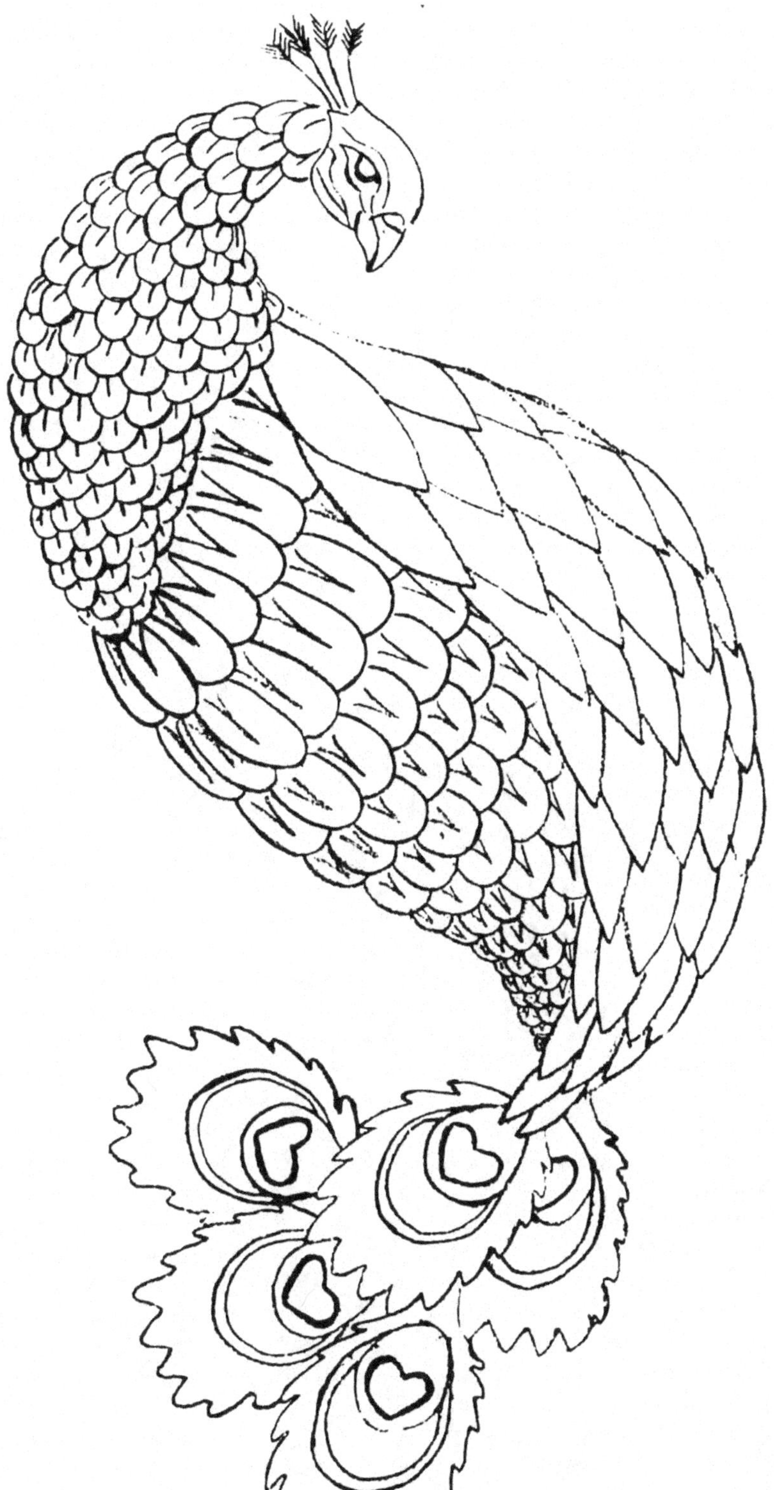

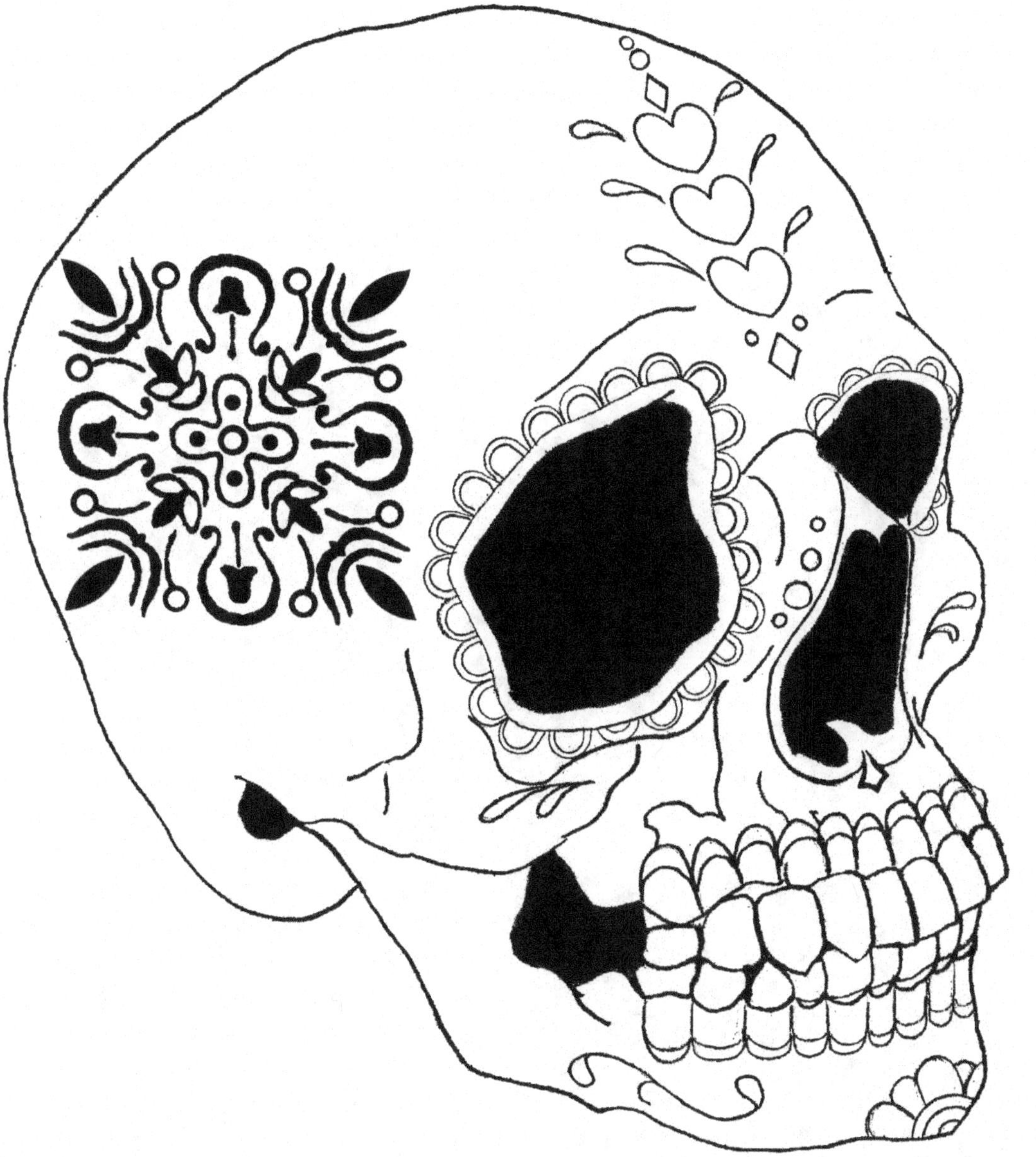

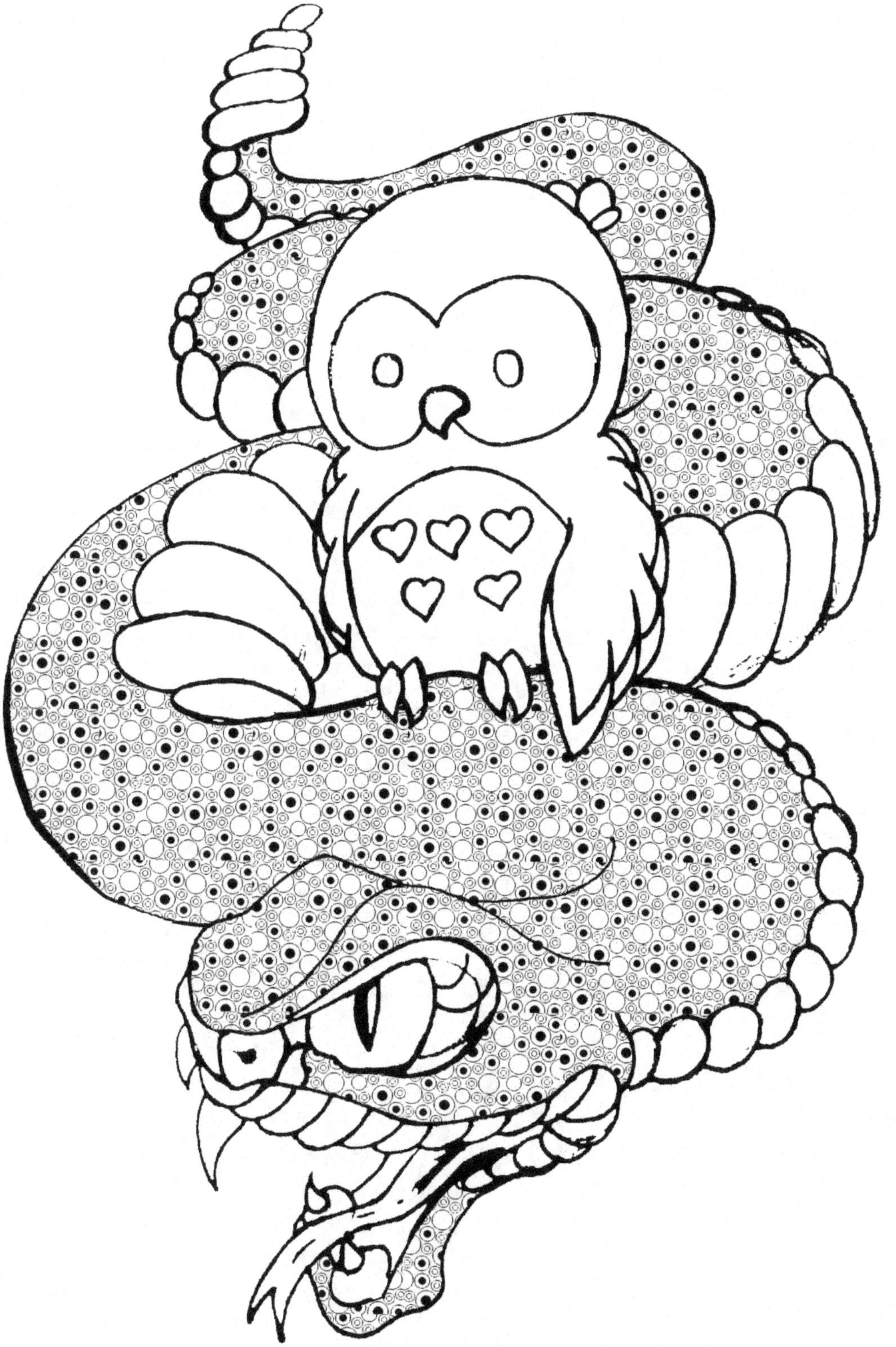

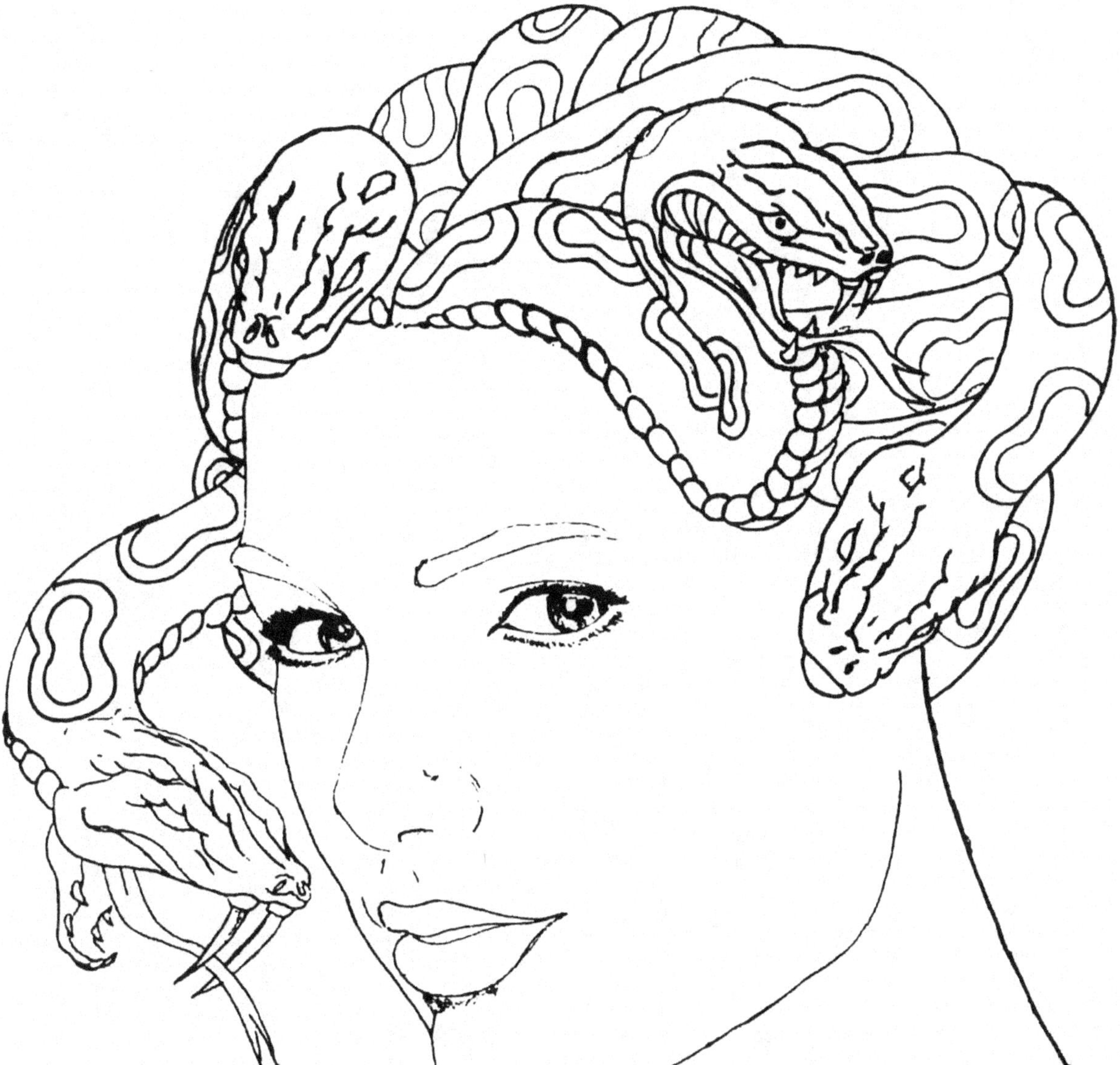

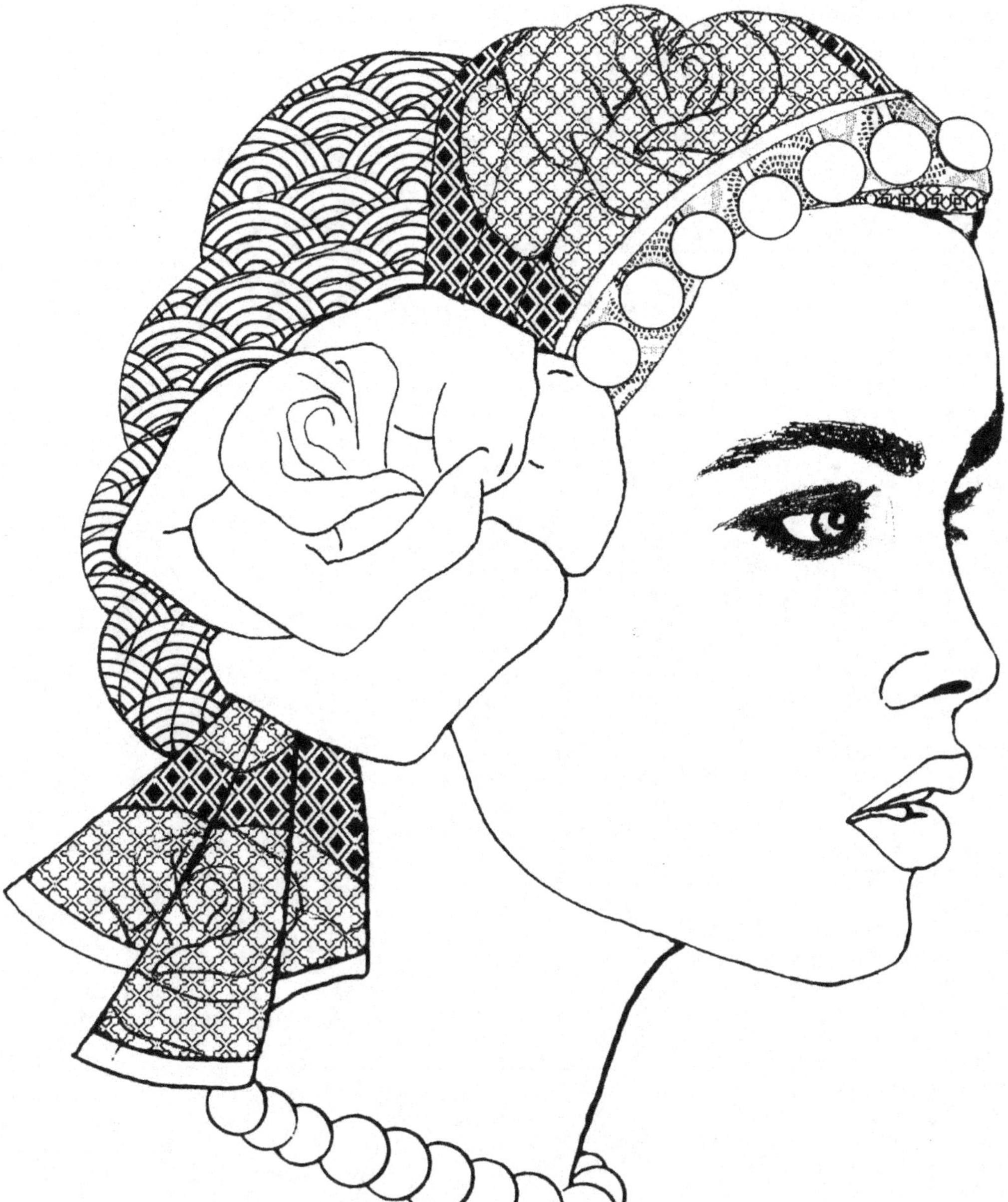

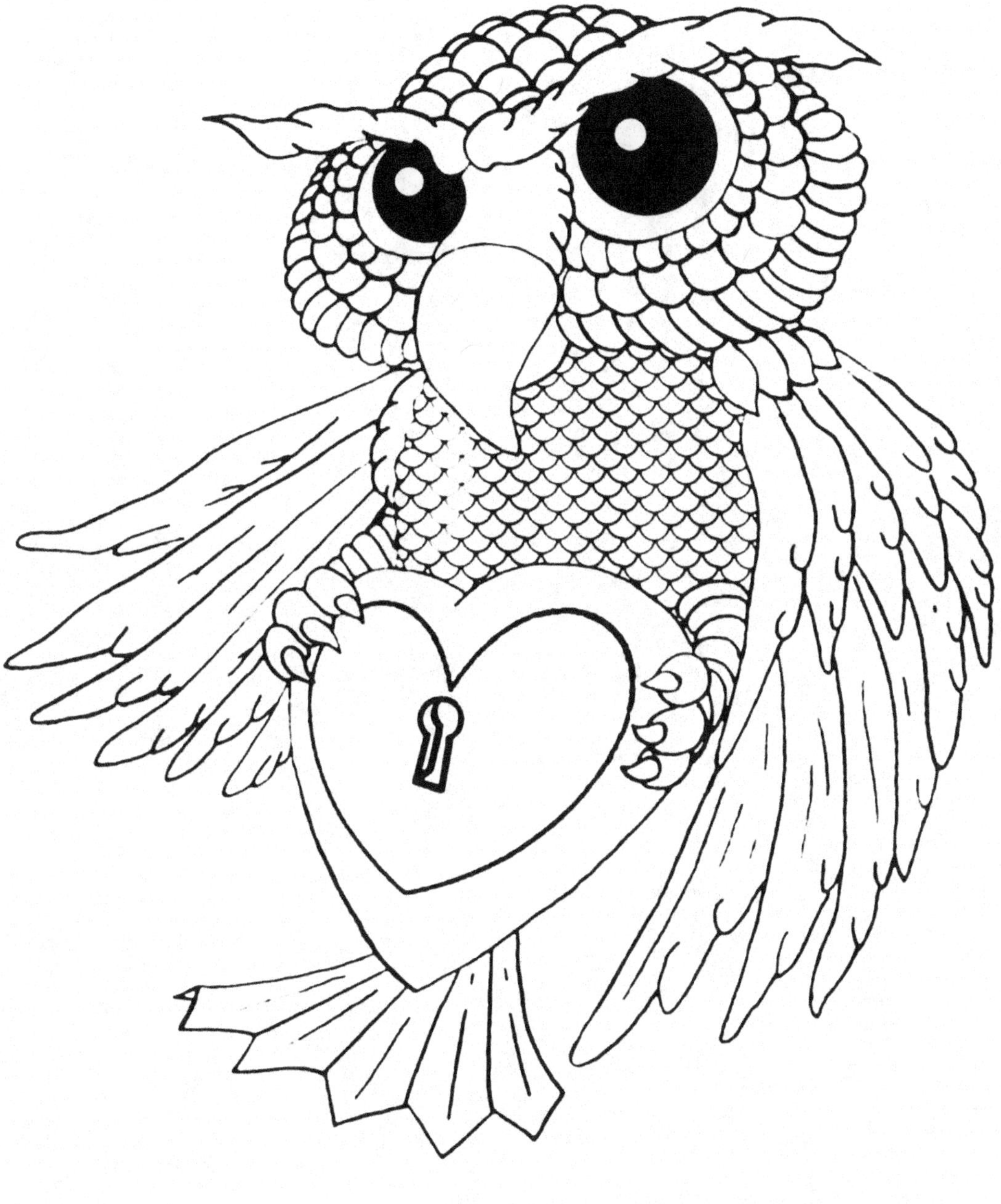

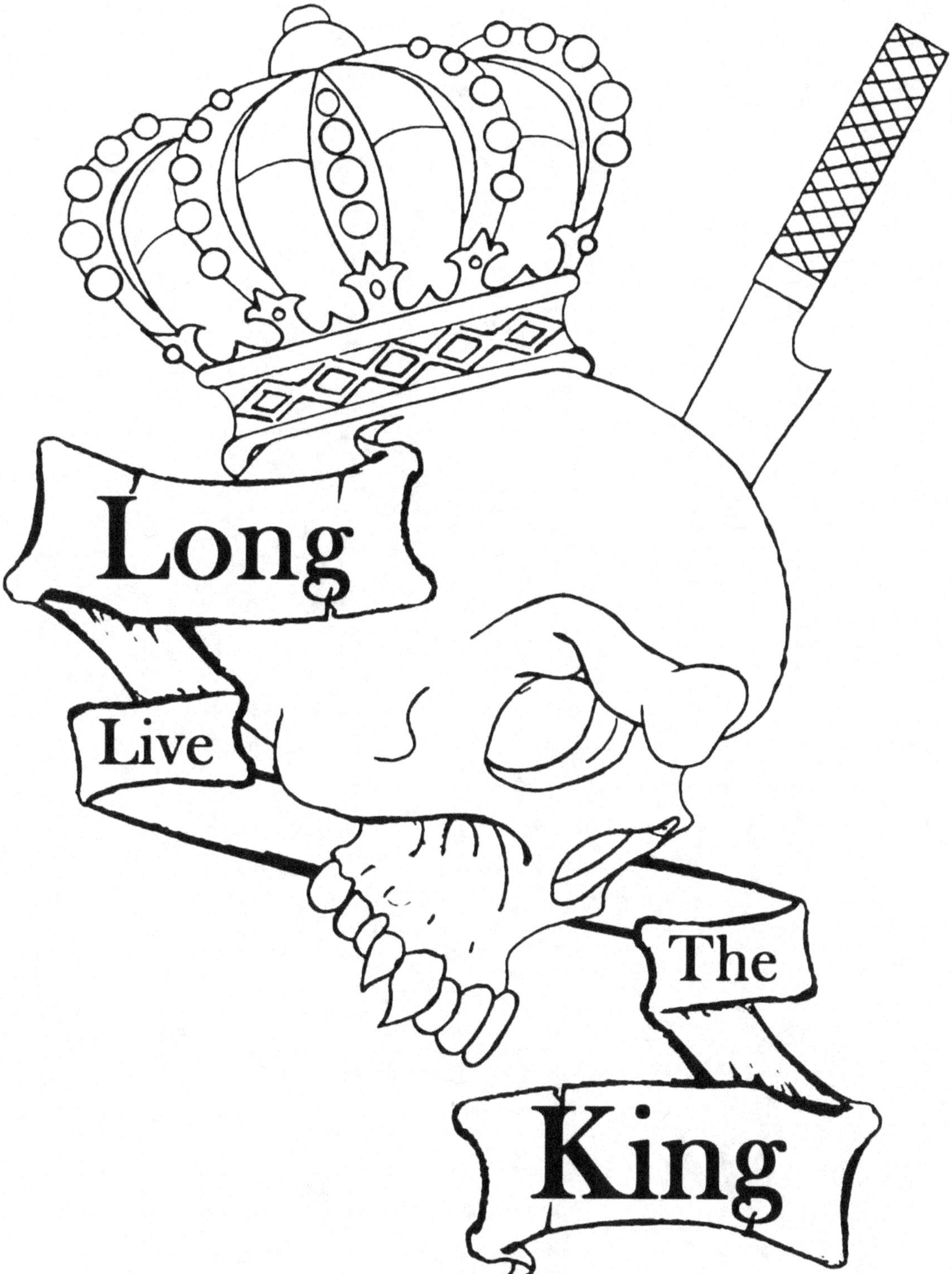
Long
Live
The
King

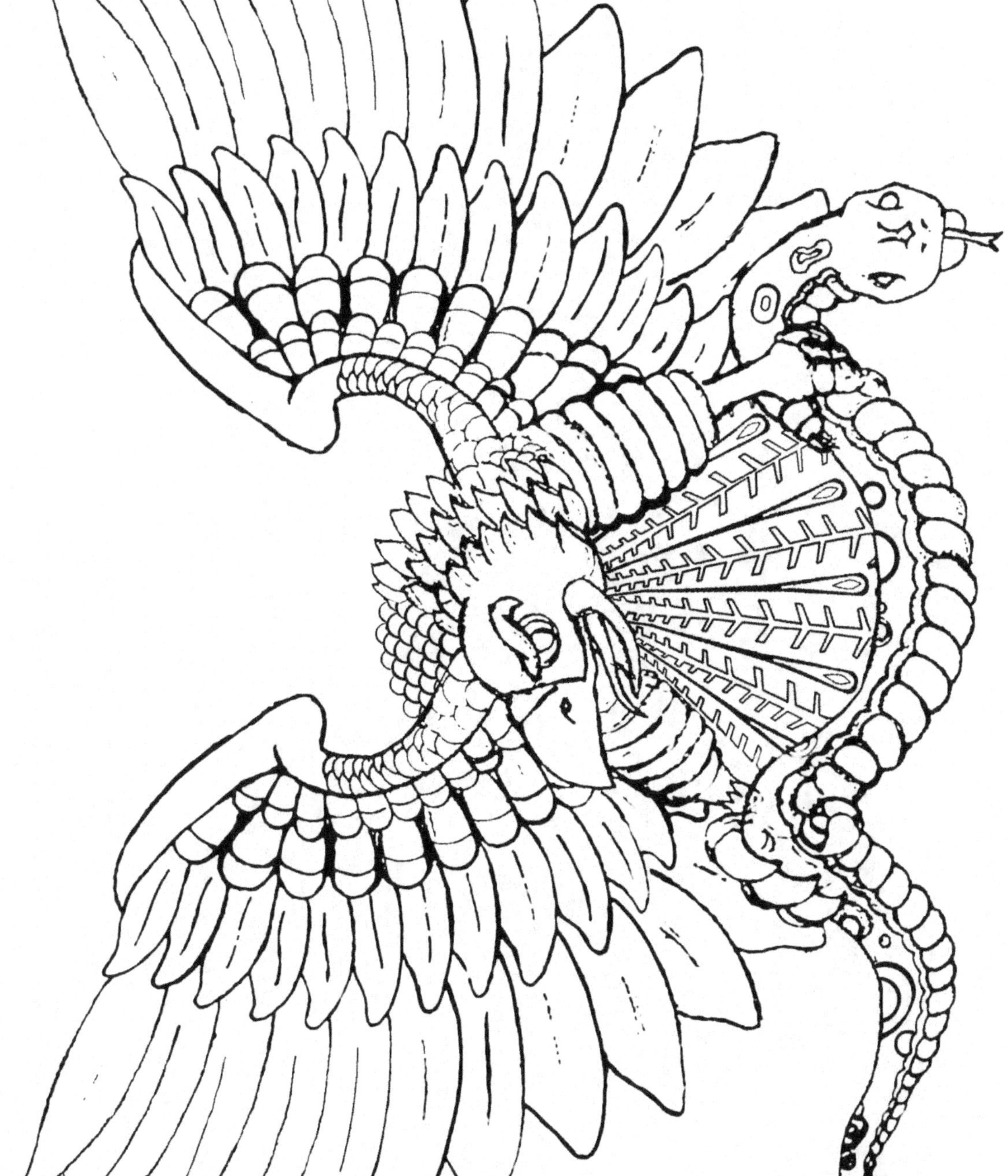

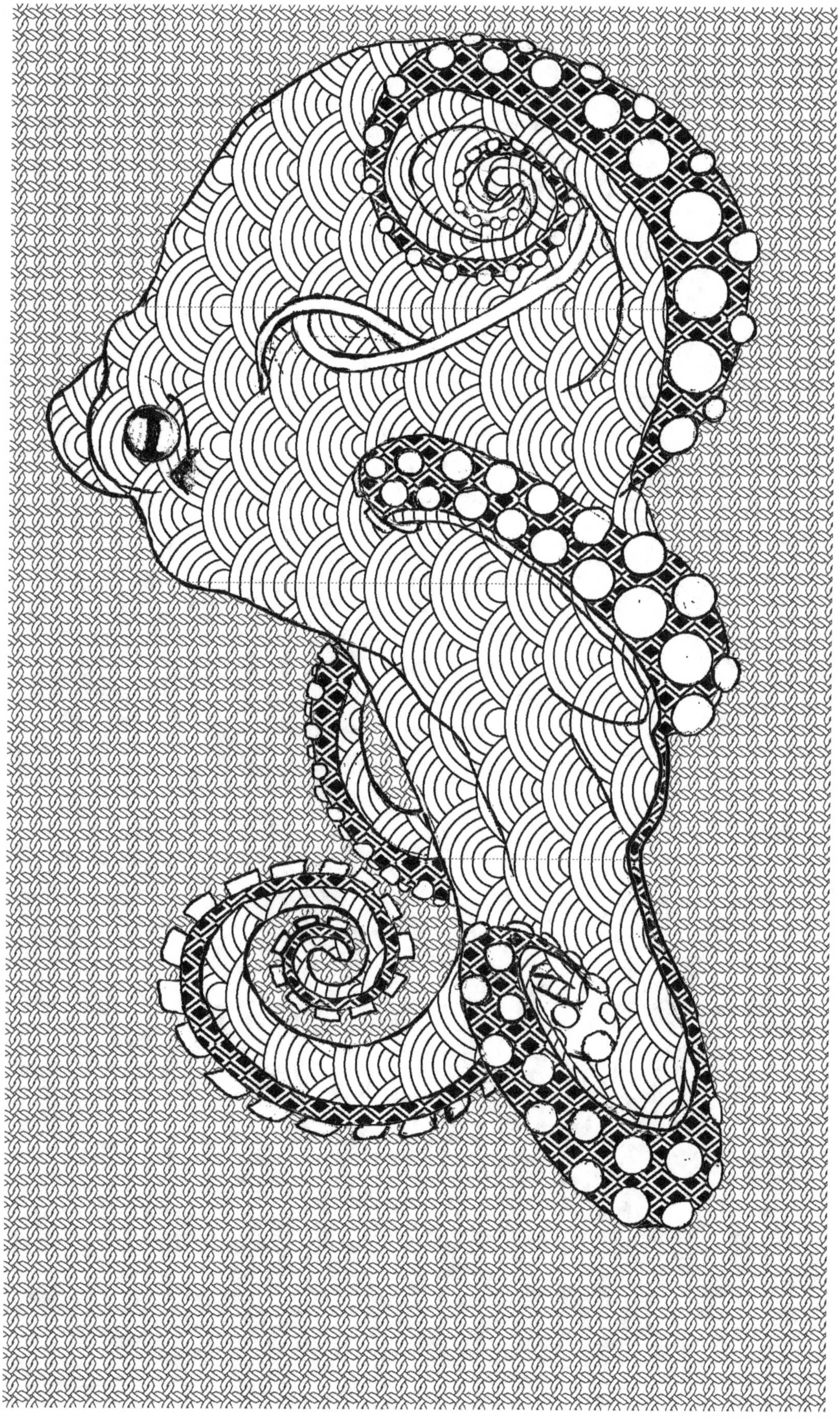

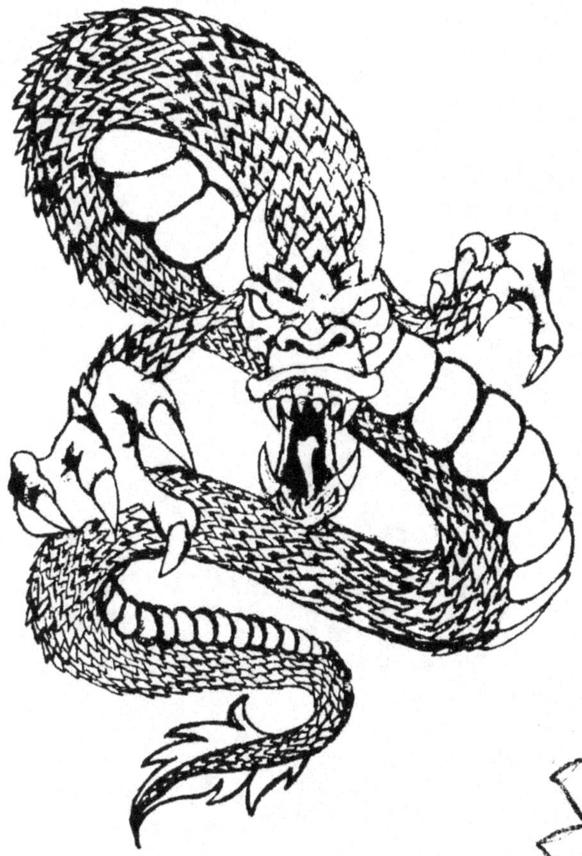

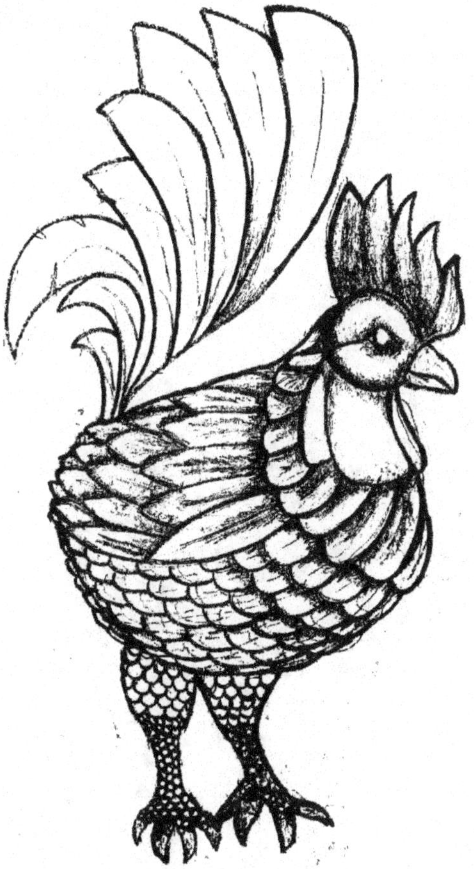

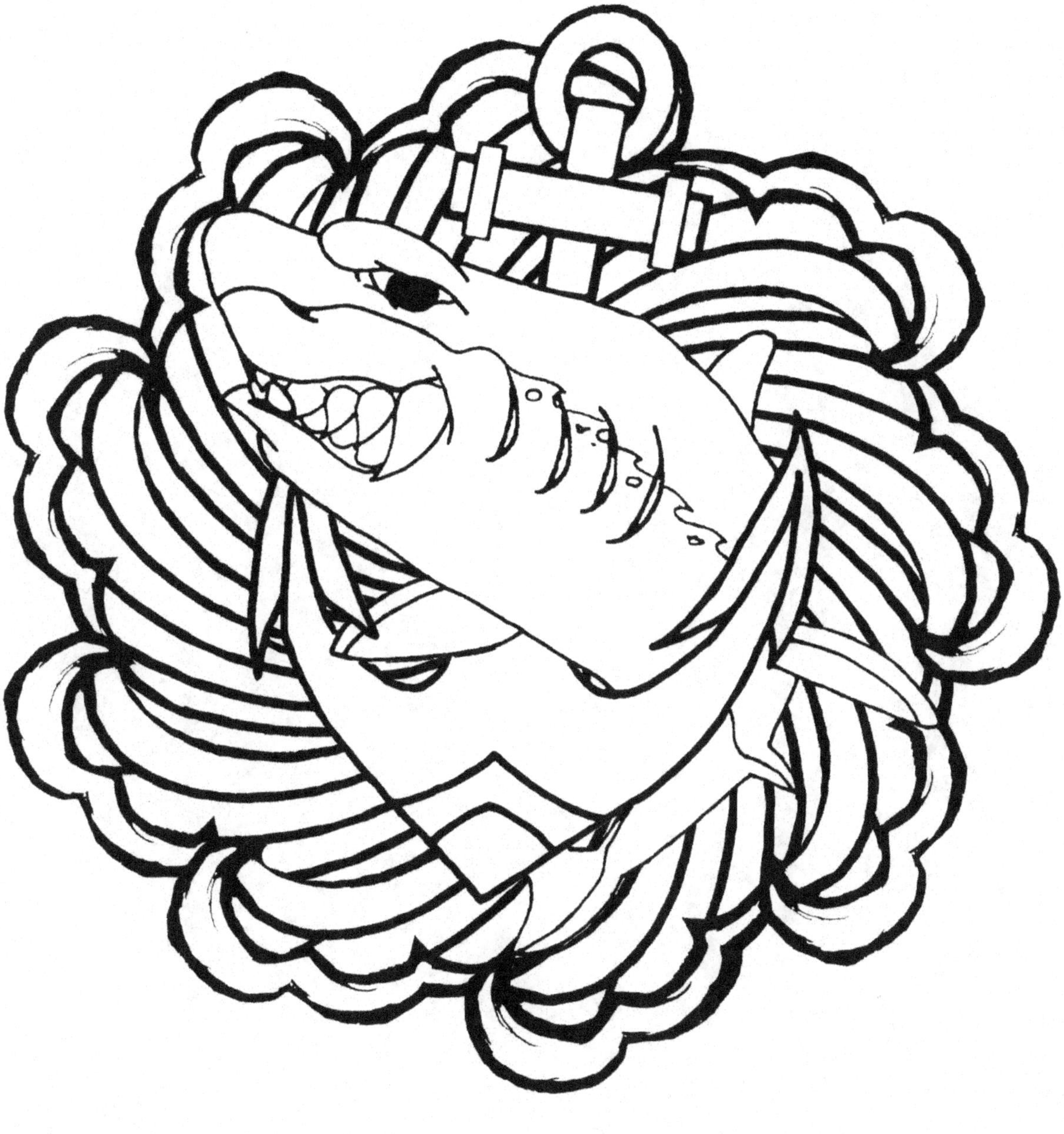

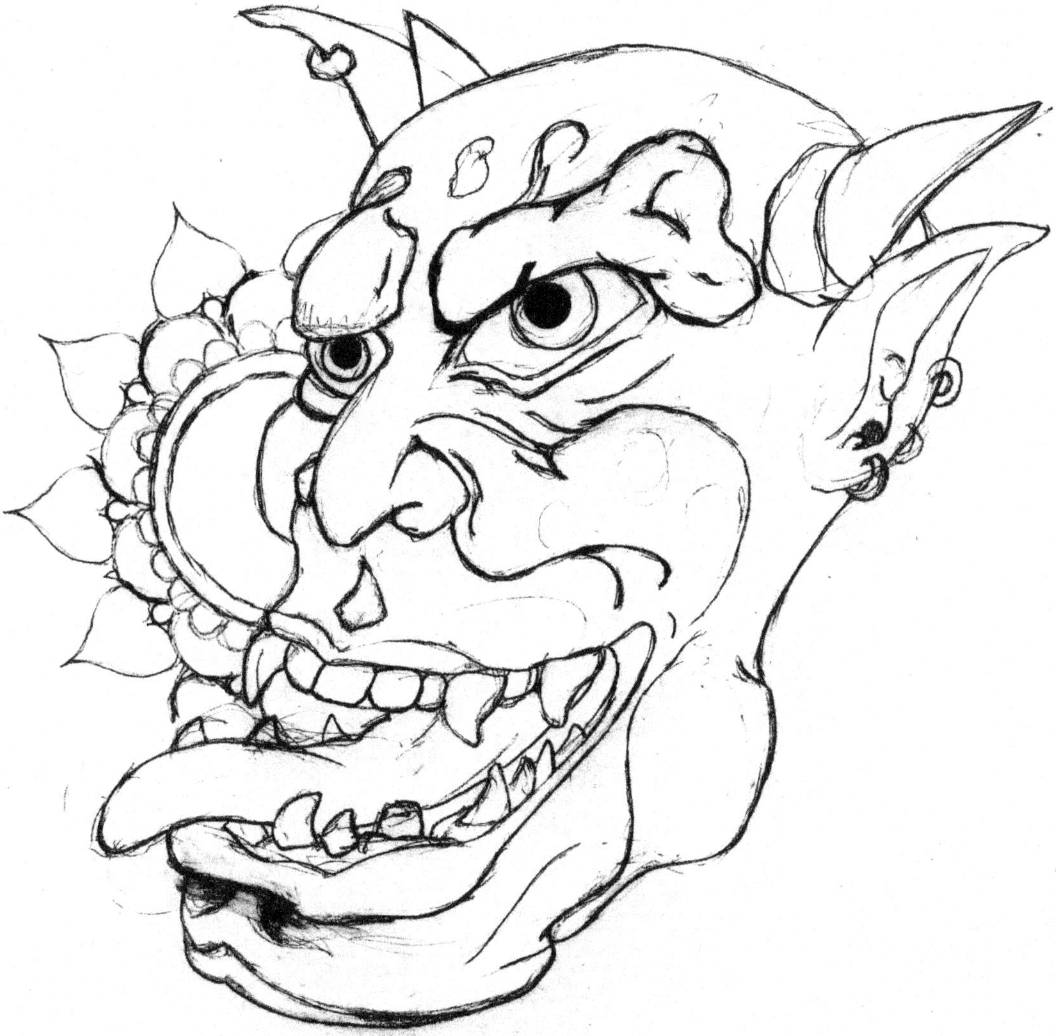

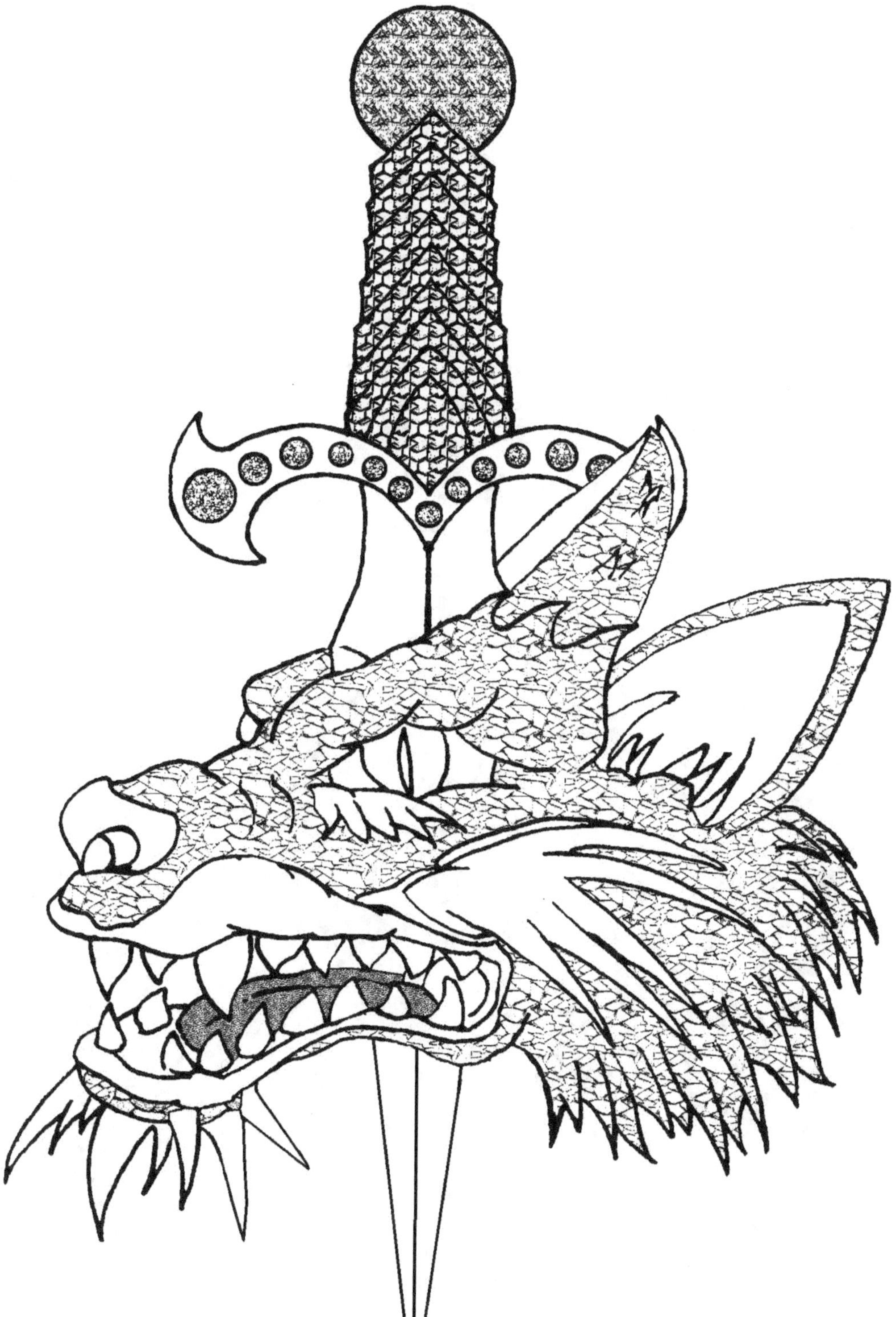

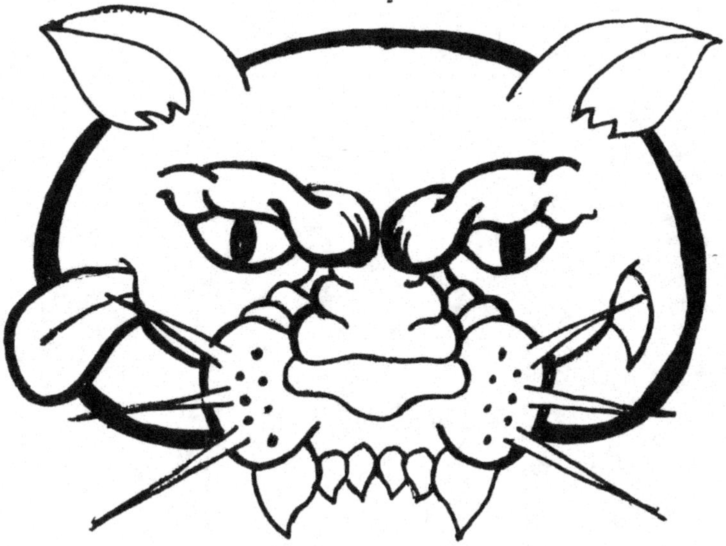

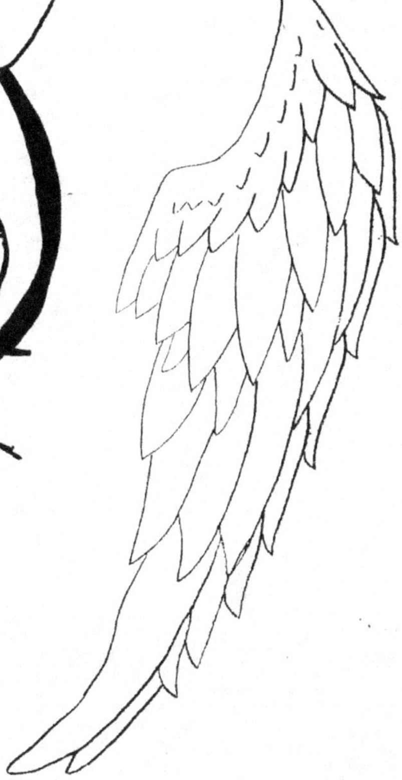

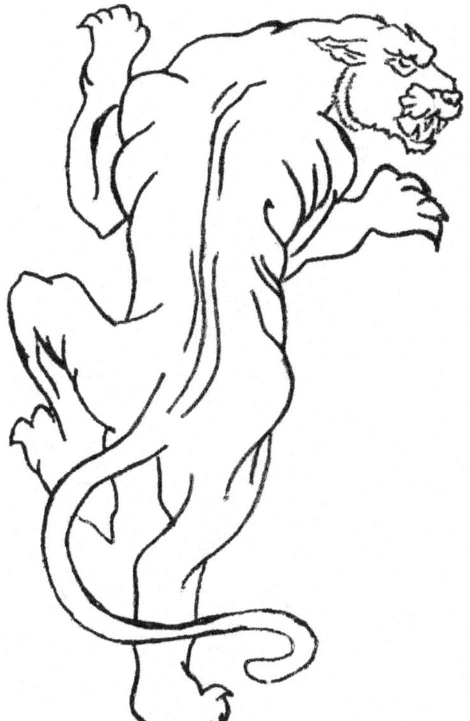

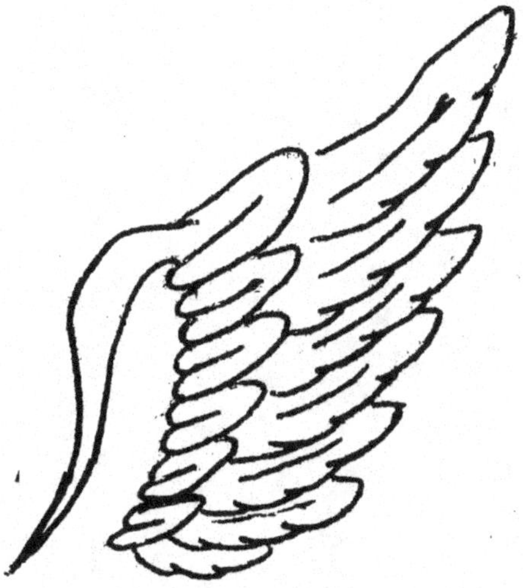

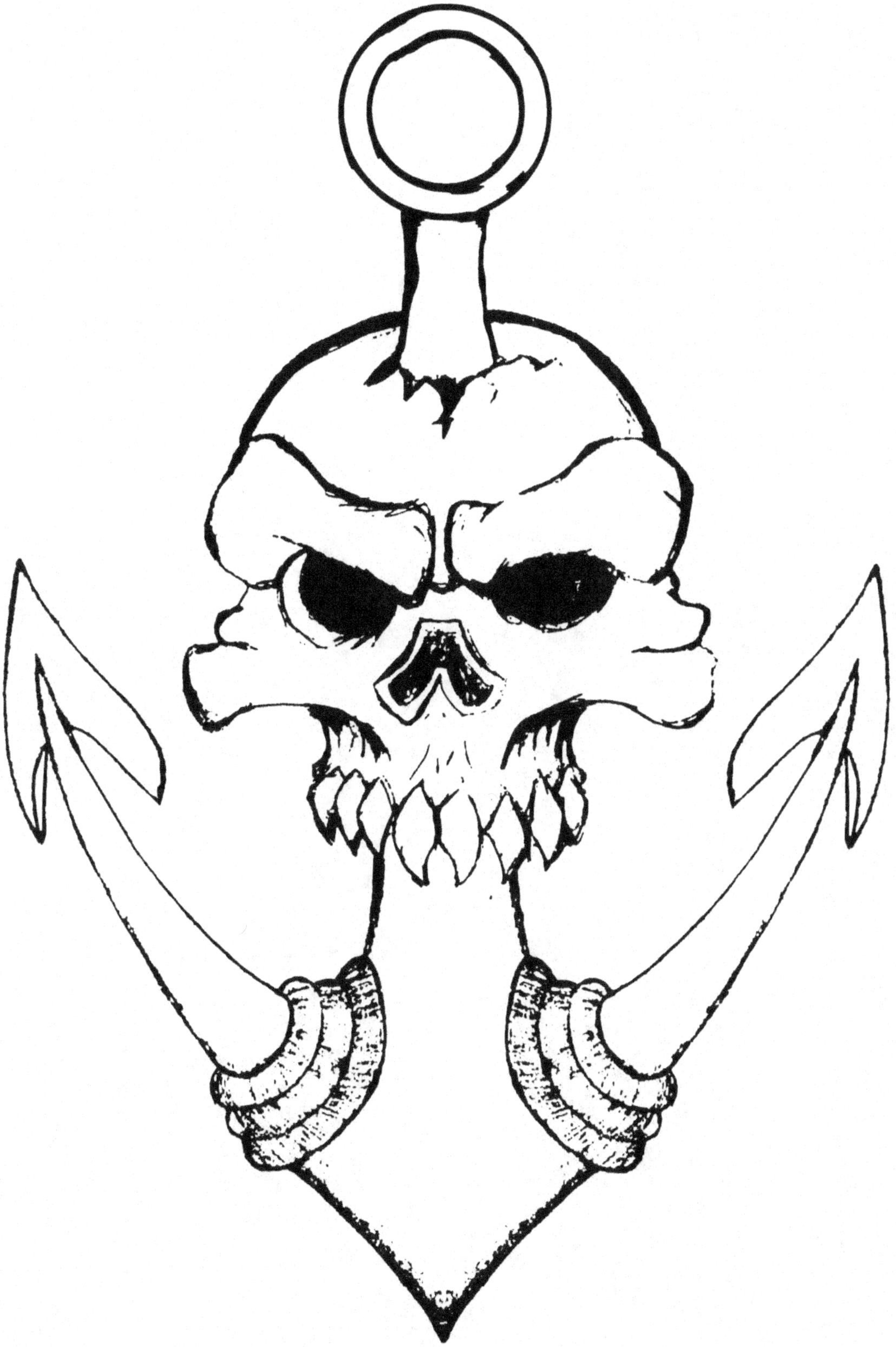

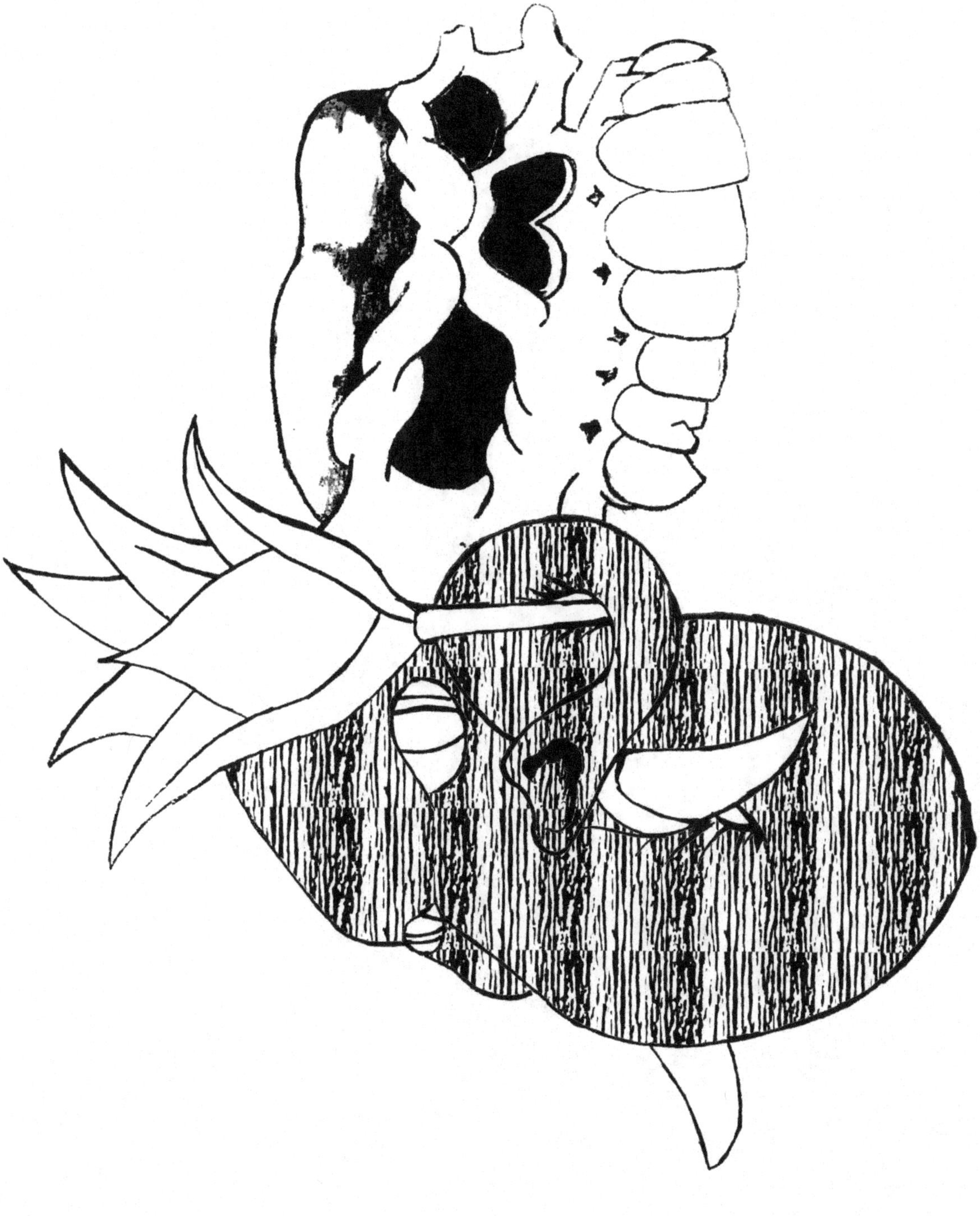

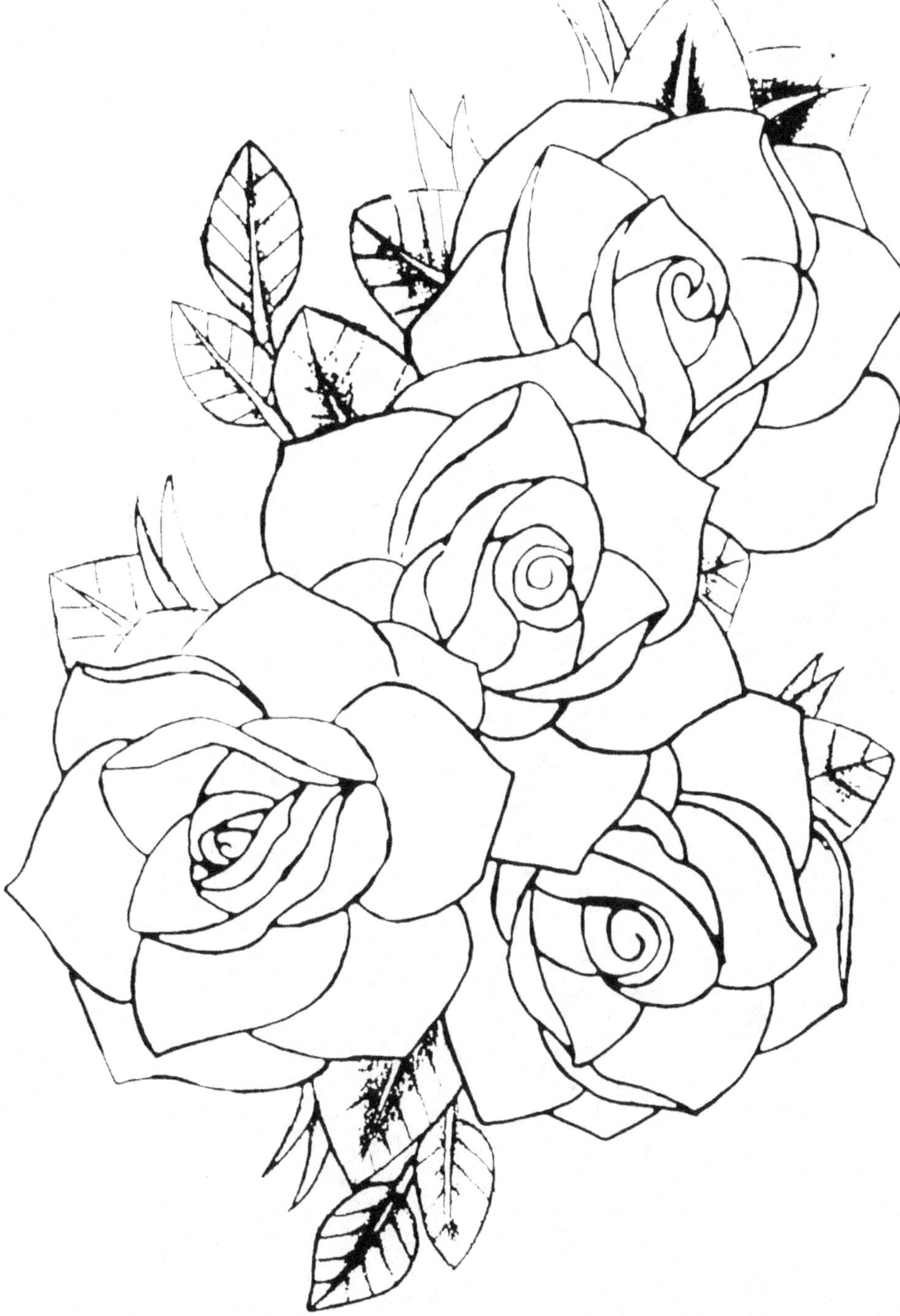

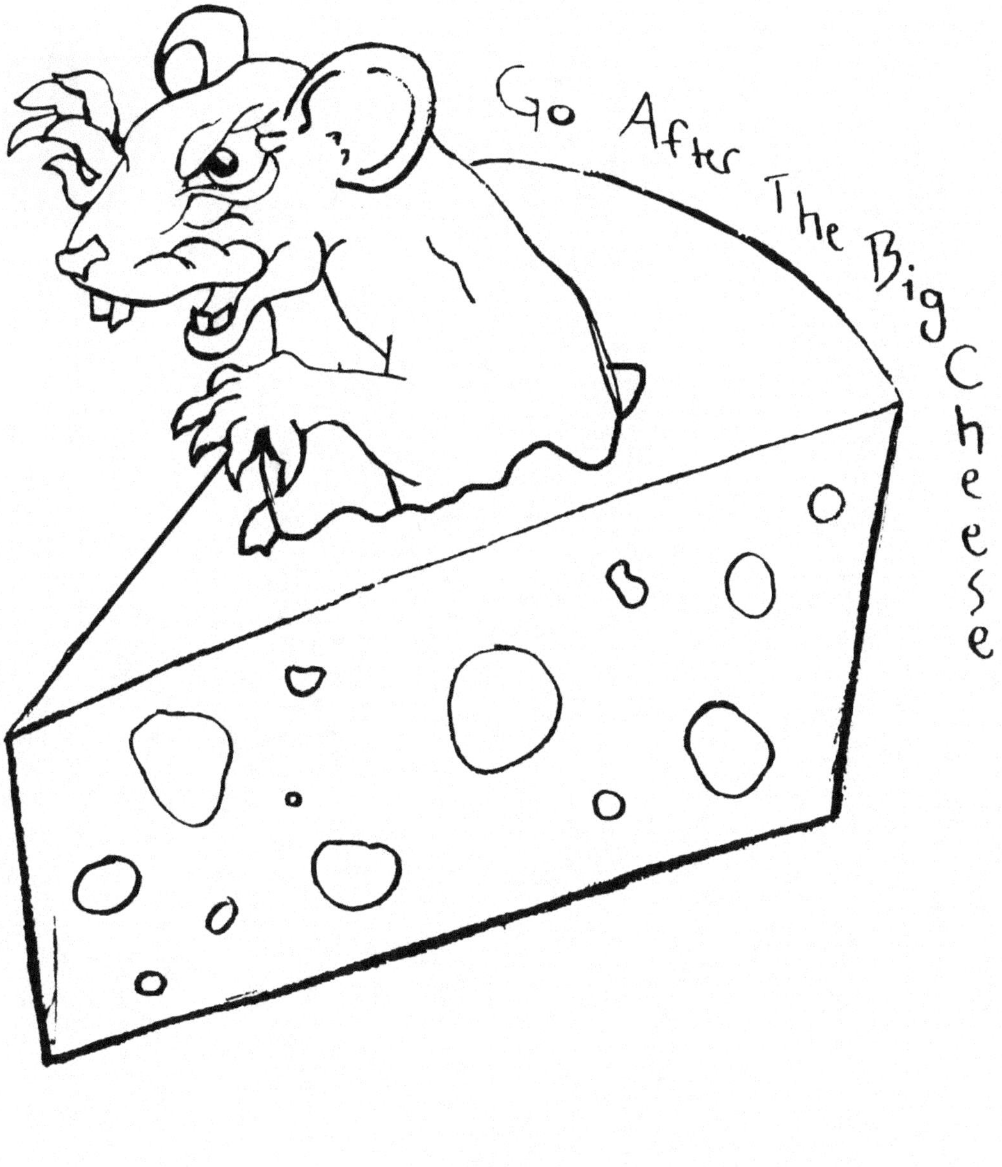
Go After The Big Cheese

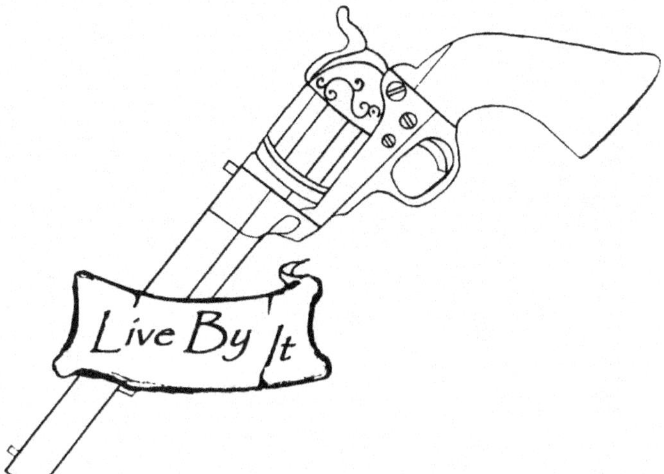
Live By It

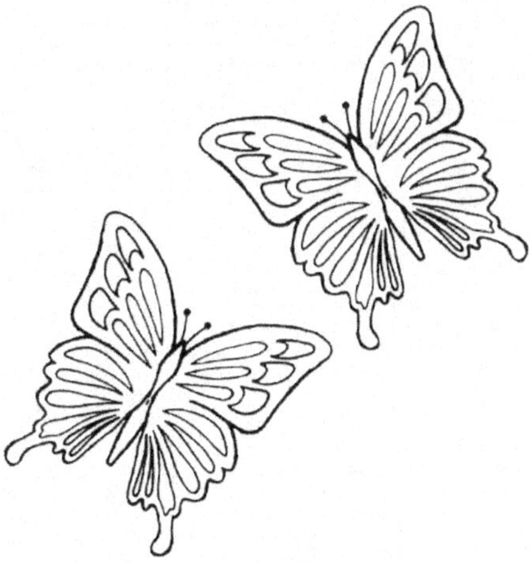

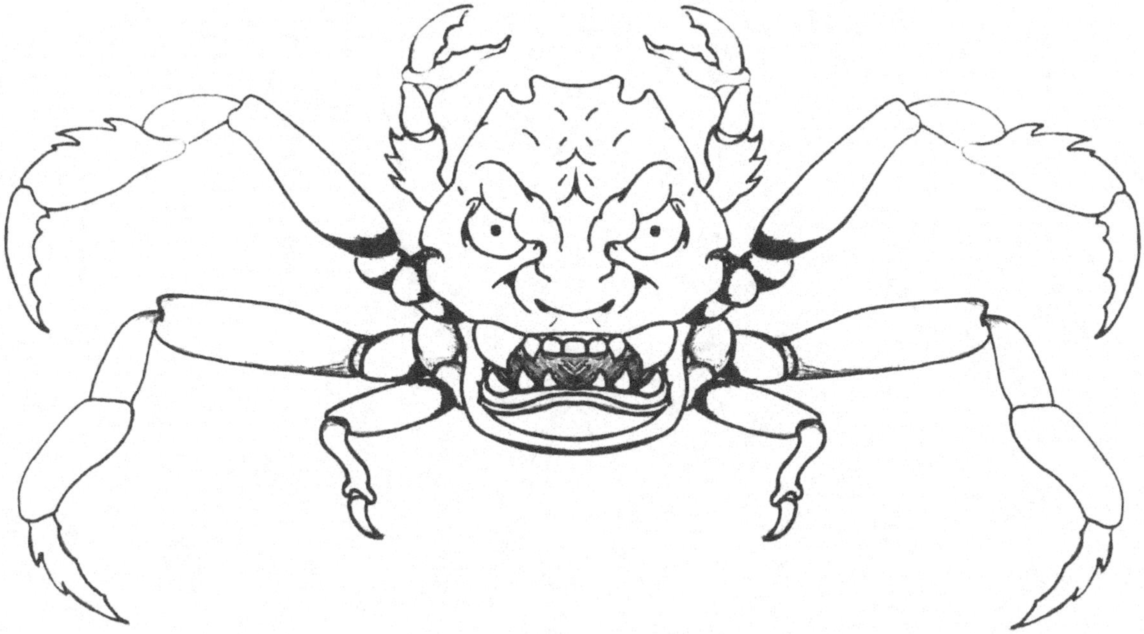

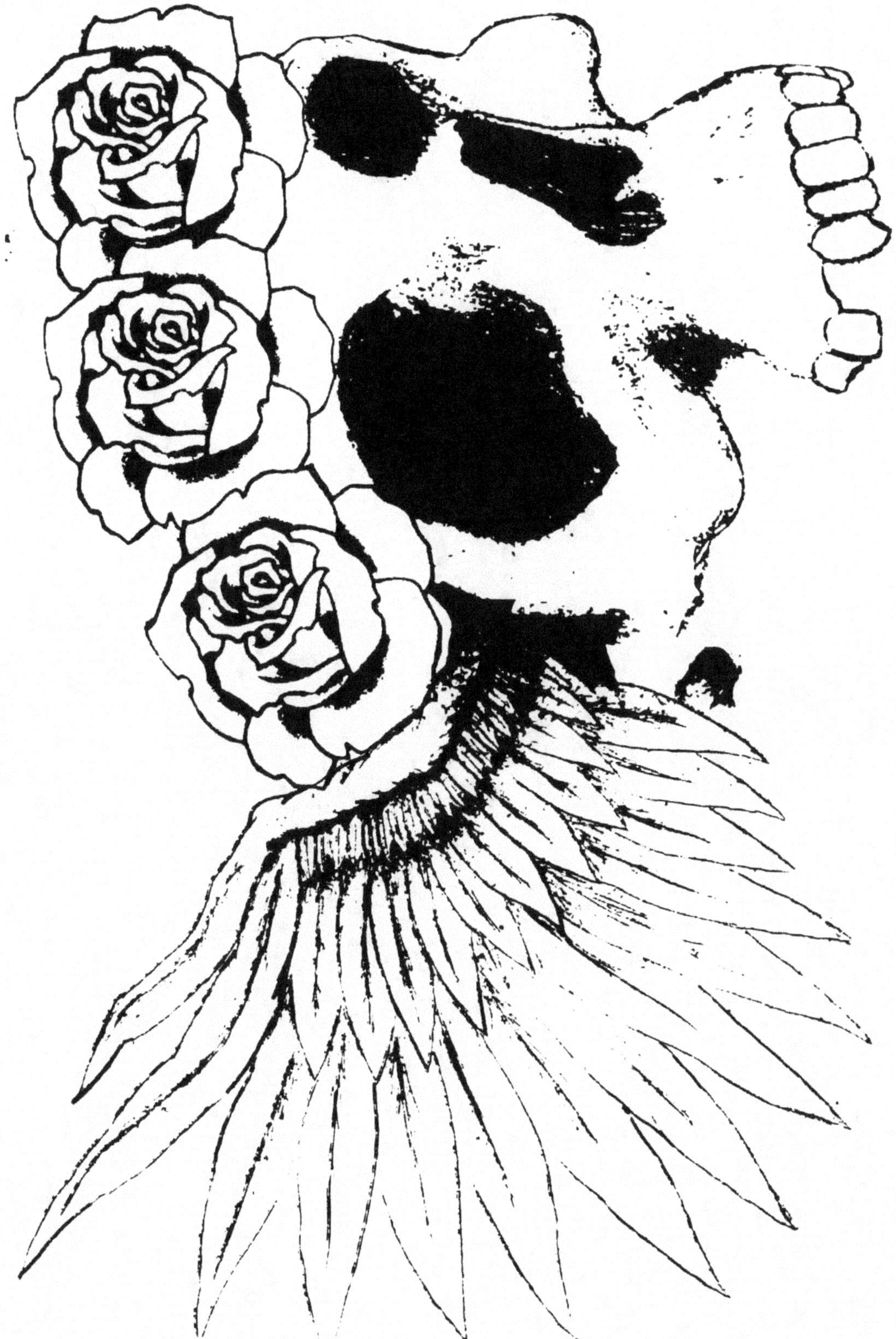

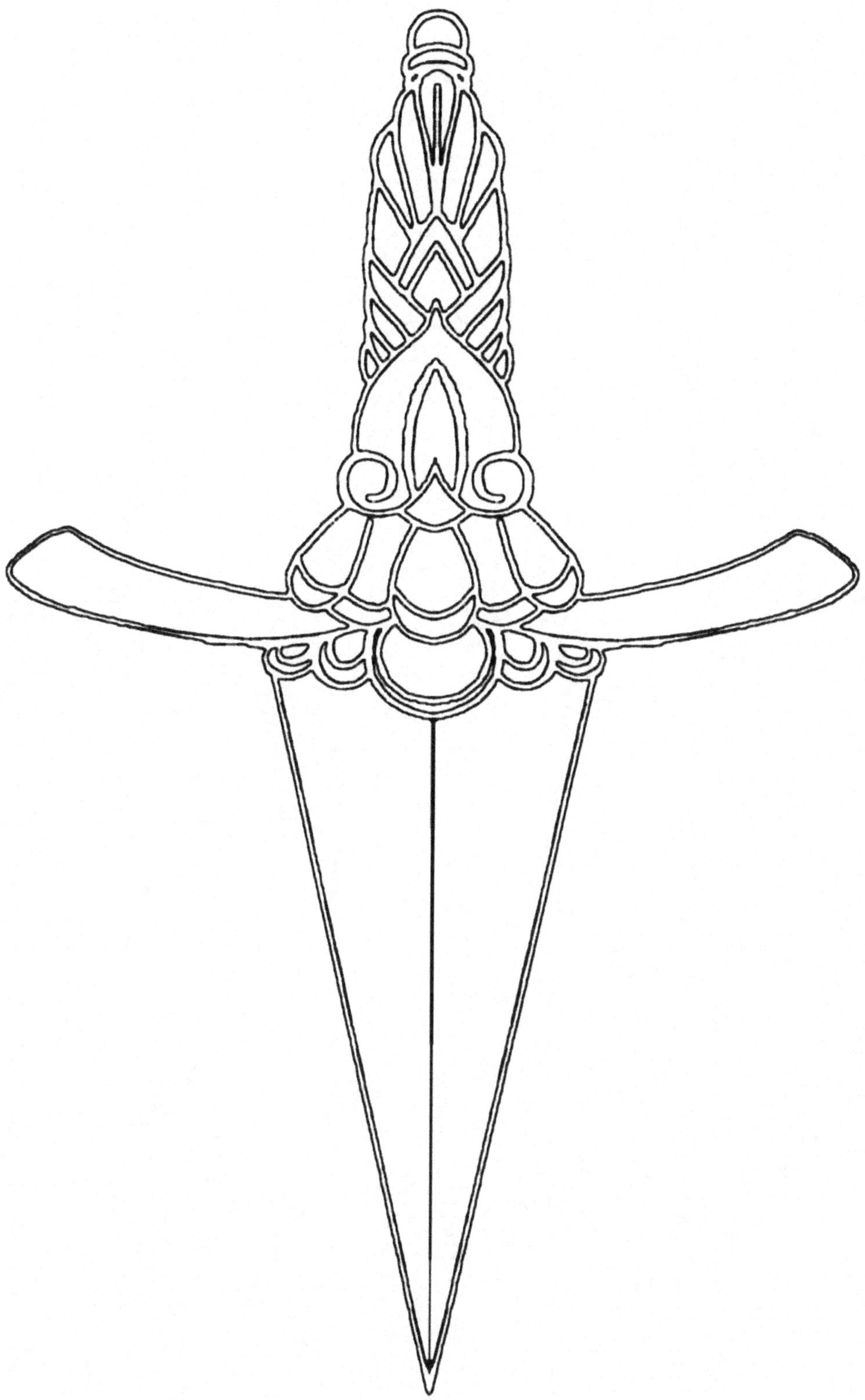

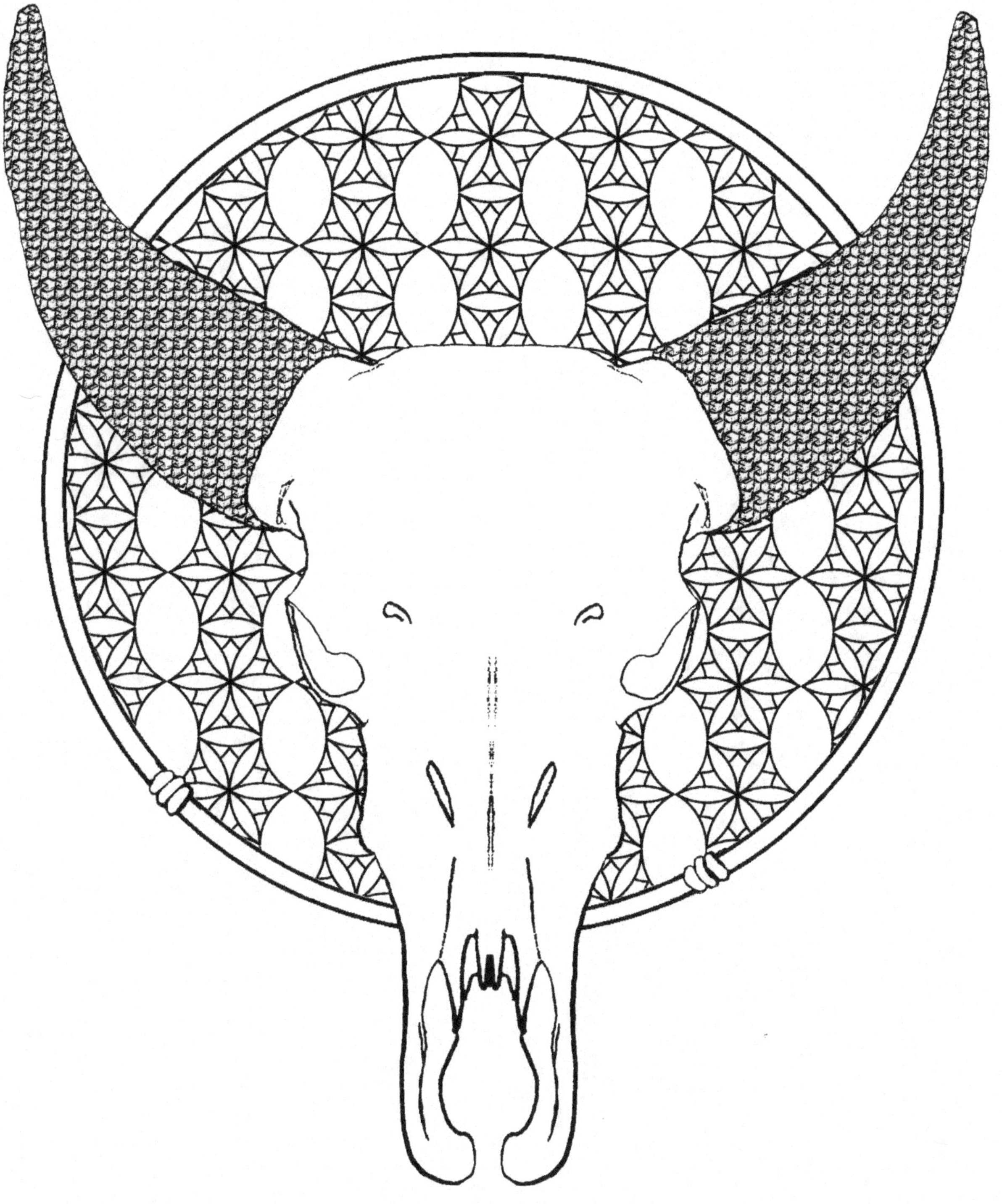

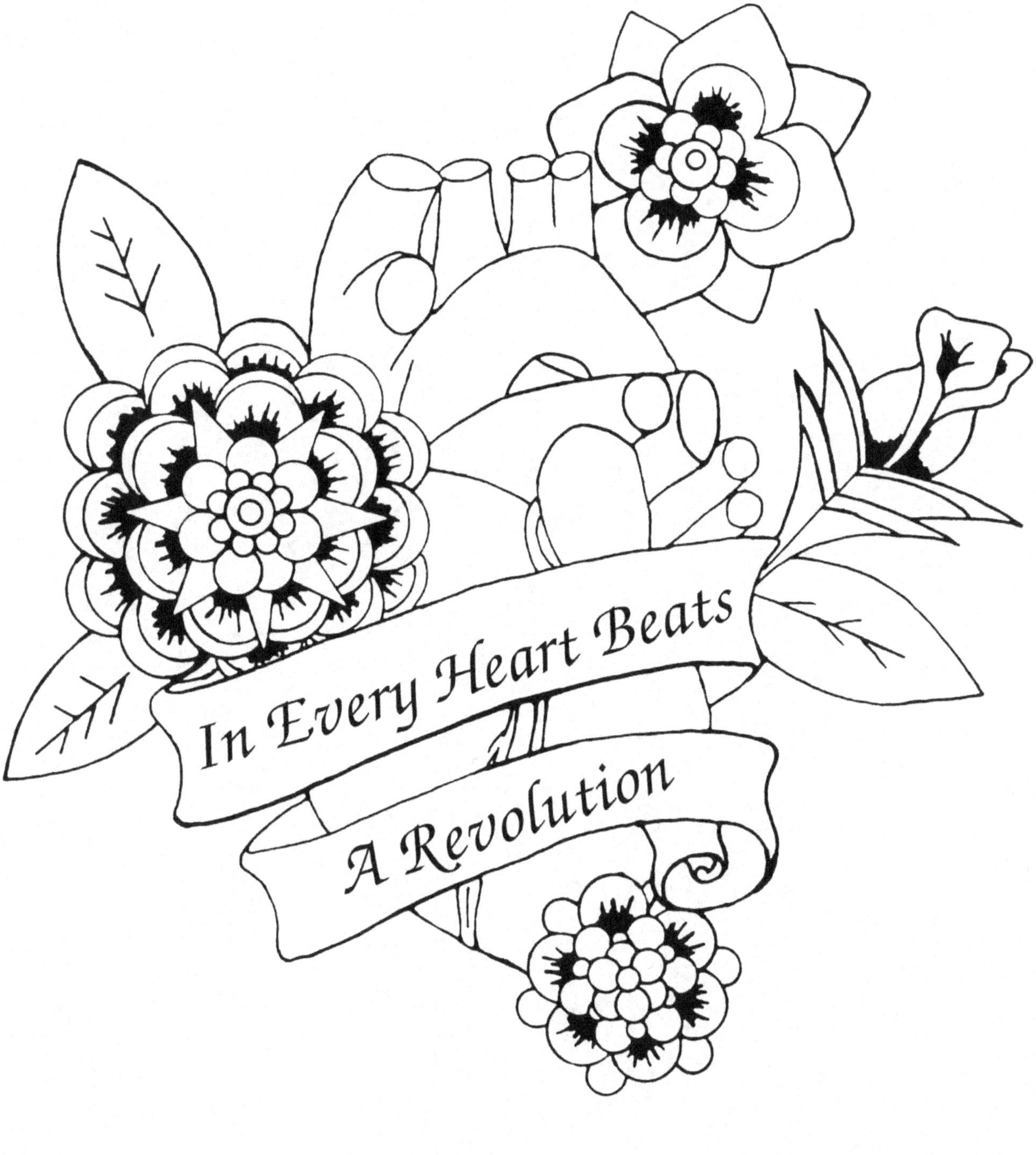
In Every Heart Beats
A Revolution

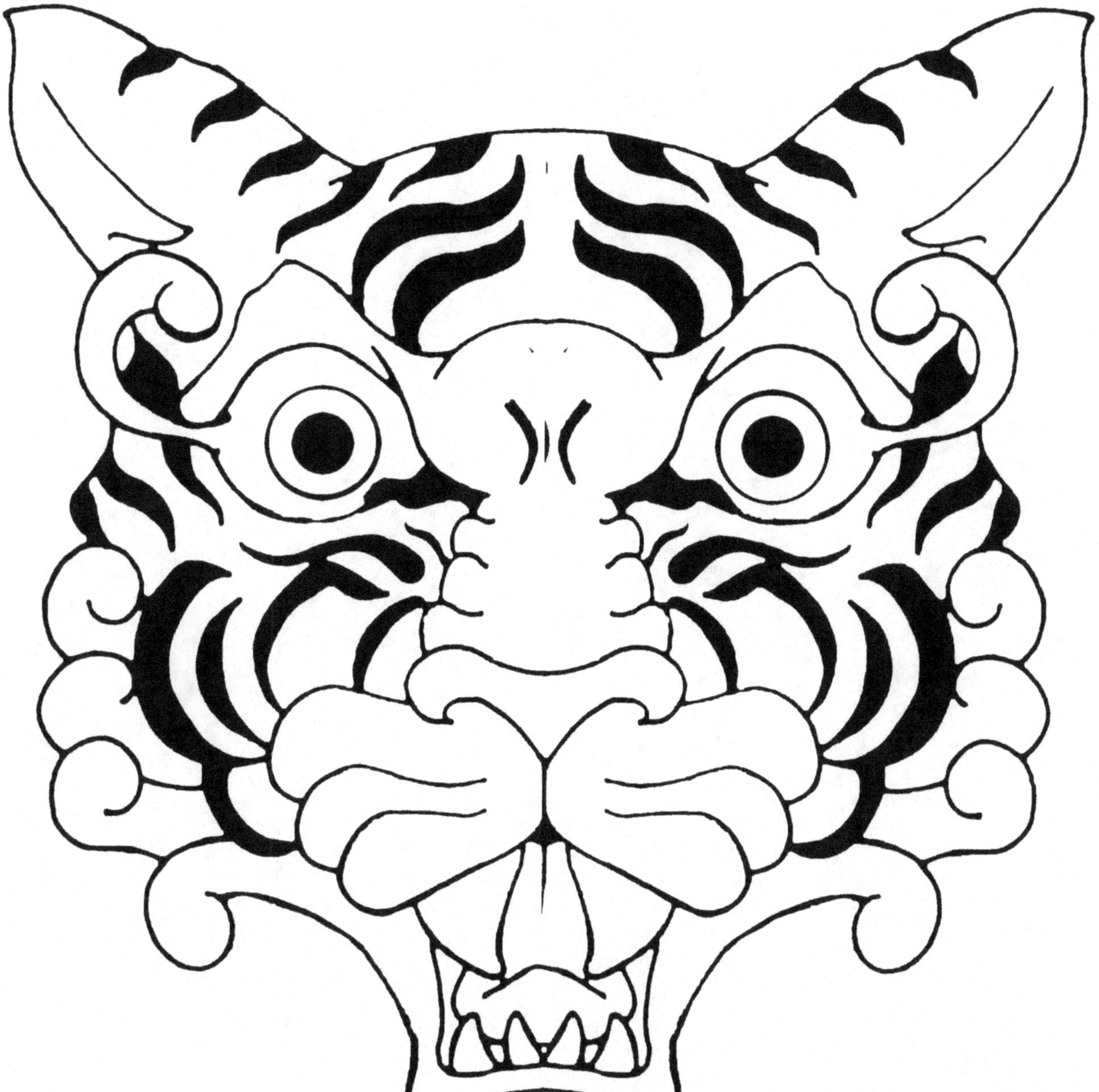

www.ingramcontent.com/pod-product-compliance
Lightning Source LLC
Chambersburg PA
CBHW081018240526
45471CB00017B/3414
* 9 7 8 1 9 8 6 6 7 9 4 2 8 *